WHITE GOLD

THE JOHN CLIFFORD STORY

by

John A. Stevens

and

Elliott Kaufmann

Published by

1 Main Street Burnstown, Ontario, Canada K0J 1G0
Telephone (613) 432-7697 Fax (613)432-7184

ISBN 0-919431-72-0
Printed and bound in Canada

Layout Design by General Store Publishing
Cover Design by Leanne Enright

Copyright © 1993
The General Store Publishing House
Burnstown, Ontario, Canada

Canadian Cataloguing in Publication Data
Stevens, John A.; Kaufmann, Elliott, 1949 -
   White Gold : the John Clifford story

ISBN 0-919431-72-0

1. Stevens, John A., 1949 –.   2. Skis and skiing – Canada.
3. Skiers – Canada – Biography.

GV854.2.C54A3 1993   796.93'2'092   C93 – 090503 – 2

First Printing November 1993

TABLE OF CONTENTS

FORWARD

There can be no denying that John Clifford is a man cut from a different bolt of cloth. He has a truly extraordinary determination that gives rise to bulldog tenacity and a persistent, evergreen optimism that oft-times appears to stretch beyond the bounds of reality.

So that, in July he'll be thinking winter, and will utter painful reminders that the days are getting shorter; in snowless Winters he'll mention a huge snowstorm out in Colorado, or Alberta, and mention that it's "supposed to be coming our way."

Supported by these virtues, John views the world through his own very personal prism, and is able to see the future, and the past, on his own terms. And that is this book.

These indomitable characteristics are what enabled John Clifford to leave the biggest footprints ever left by man in the Gatineau Hills. He developed the Ottawa Ski Club's home at Camp Fortune, he developed Mont Ste. Marie, he developed Mont Cascades. He was responsible for the since abandoned ski facilities at Beamishill in the Gatineau, and Carlington Park in Ottawa.

As a newspaperman in Ottawa for 40 years, I was in a position to observe John at close range through most of his career.

A list of his accomplishments fills pages, and as a native of Ottawa, a former ski champion and still a champion ski-builder, it is entirely appropriate that his story be told and that posterity be served.

From his latest mountaintop perch at Mount Pakenham, John has set down his highlights, and how they were achieved, in a long and fruitful career.

Views from the outside, especially over so many years, may differ from event to event, and so this book is a particularly interesting and valuable read because it affords us a view of the tumult from the eye of the storm.

It is a story that had to be told because John's career has had an impact on so many thousands of people. Those who have witnessed even tiny fragments of his involvement in skiing will surely find this book interesting and enjoyable.

Eddie MacCabe

PROLOGUE

Portillo Chile, 1946 – Johnny Clifford stood awestruck as the world champion disappeared 1500 feet below him, leaving a vapour trail of fine-blown snow on the highest, steepest ski run the young Canadian had ever seen.

John was next. He had come 10,000 miles on guts and a shoestring to compete with the best skiers in the western hemisphere. This was the next big challenge in his adventurous life. A three thousand foot drop at unprecedented speed.

Drawing together all his resources of courage, determination, and skill, he focused himself, gritted his teeth and launched himself into the unknown.

CHAPTER 1
Canada's One Man Ski Team

Information on Chilean skiing is scarce. It is all open skiing above timber, you climb steadily hour after hour before you finally take off your skins and come down, and powder snow is more the rule than the exception. If time is short you'll want to make Santiago your headquarters. It's the starting point for more snow fields than any other city. Pack mules must be obtained for the final stage of your trip up into the snow and a nominal sum will reserve you a bunk at a club refuge. You must be prepared to walk, climb, ride muleback or jolt along in a truck as circumstances demand. This is a distinct advantage. It saves the Andes for skiers only.

This description is from the American Ski Annual of 1938-39. There was very little change by 1946; World War II had kept South American skiing in a dormant state. In an attempt to bring some order to world class competition the Ski Union of the Americas was formed. The first post-war South American venture into international competitive skiing came with the Hemispheric Championships, to be held in Chile. South American member countries, the United States and Canada were invited to send teams.

Chilean skiing was coming out of the dark ages; transportation from Santiago to the Andean snowfields was still by narrow gauge railway but it was now possible for the skier to get to the Refugio in Portillo with relative ease and comfort. Transportation from the Refugio to the ski area was improved with a "modern" cog railway replacing the mules or trucks that were used back in '39. Augustine Edwards,

1

the wealthy head of the Chilean Ski Federation, banker and area developer, initiated the competition to introduce Chilean skiing to the world. He still wanted to "save the Andes for skiers", but he wanted them to come in greater numbers. World class competition would put Portillo on the map, and he felt 1946 was the year to introduce the Chilean Andes to the ski world.

Much of the impetus in forming the Union came from Fred Hall, past-president of the Canadian Amateur Ski Association and the first president of the Union. He felt this meet was important not only to the C.A.S.A but to Canada as a whole. Knowing the primitive conditions promised to any foreign team and with Canada's ski funds non-existant, he was about to regretfully decline the invitation when the Alpine Chairman of the C.A.S.A, John Clifford, volunteered to go. The volunteer received the association's backing – official but not financial. Clifford decided to go as a delegate and to compete as well. He began by hitchhiking to New York.

He was not alone at the start of the journey; George Grossman was also lifting his thumb on the road. George, an "A" class skier with a few wins under his belt, also wanted to represent Canada at this prestigious South American event. He had been accepted as a participant, but he was not a delegate. George was not shy; his pleading look stopped cars whenever he made eye contact with an oncoming driver. A few years younger than John, he had the same world-beating ambitions; he thought he also had the same fortitude.

They left Ottawa in the early hours of the morning, each with a packsack on his back and ski boots slung over his shoulder. Reaching Albany, N.Y. late the same afternoon, with many more miles to go to get to the big city, they boarded a bus to complete the trip.

That night, as John slipped between the damp sheets of the dingy four-dollar-a-night hotel on Manhattan's 8th Avenue and 42nd Street, he thought back on how he had arrived at this point in his life, the vivid memories flashing through his tired mind: ski races of the past, downhill, slalom and cross-country, particularly those he had not won; recollections of the Night Riders of Camp Fortune, where it all started. Sleep eluded him, and after a restless eternity of self-doubt, morning arrived, bringing with it the problems of the next leg of the journey. With only $100 between them they had to act quickly.

As luck would have it, their hotel was just around the corner from one of the many store-front employment agencies of the time. All types of jobs were listed on the posters hung in the windows. The job market was good and the choice was theirs. Not knowing how far away Coney Island was, John chose to work for a Dairy Queen. It was a long subway ride out to work and back, but as it was night work it suited him; his days were free to search for a ship going to South America. George went to work as a salad chef in a night club restaurant closer to home on Broadway: all the salad he could eat, and the occasional glimpse of the stars Ray Everly and Helen O'Connell were his perks. The pay was pretty good too; he couldn't earn $250 a week in Ottawa!

The answer was the same at all of the shipping company offices that they visited: "South America? Nope – how about Africa or England or Alaska?" Working passage was available to just about anywhere except where they wanted to go; time was passing, days turning into weeks. The hot concrete of summer in Manhattan was hell for the two young ski racers yearning for the snowy slopes of Chile.

After weeks of looking they stumbled upon the tiny well-hidden office of a Chilean shipping line. Here they were told of a new Swedish ship, the 5,000 ton **Atomena**, leaving for Chile the next day, and actually looking for two extra hands.

The ship's hiring officer looked tough, with his unshaven face, dirty white shirt and stained bell-bottom trousers. Recognizing their anxiety, he drove a hard bargain. He offered John the position of purser's helper and George that of ordinary seaman, a deckhand. They were only to be paid if the Captain liked the quality of their work. Dismissing the thought that they might be put ashore in some foreign port, short of their destination, at the whim of a dissatisfied Captain, they signed on.

They left the small dockside office, trading the salty smell of the port for the stench of the New York subway system, returning to Flea-bag Manor for the last time. John was at the top of the hill with another challenging run ahead of him. "Course!" he shouted, as he pushed his way through the 42nd Street hikers and hustlers, between the subway exit and the hotel. George, however, was about to balk at the gate.

There was no question in John's mind about sailing on the Atomena, but George was concerned that he might not get back to Ottawa for the start of the new school year. His reluctance was reinforced by his boss, the chef at the nightclub. George had developed a comfortable rapport with this man, a former Swedish ski jumper. The skier-to-skier conversation during lulls in the kitchen work often dwelt on the unpleasantness of world travel.

"George, you can't quit now, not after coming this far," John repeated over and over again. Finally, as the light of dawn overpowered the flashing neon red in the room's small window, he thought he had convinced George that the trip would be worthwhile. They boarded the ship that noon. After stowing their gear in their stuffy, airless quarters below deck, they reported for duty. Minutes before sailing, George jumped ship; John was on his own.

The kit that John brought on board had expanded from the original packsack and ski boots. Wiser now in the ways of the world, he purchased cartons of cigarettes with all the cash he could scrape together, intending to resell them in South America at a profit. He was about to become Canada's first skier whose equipment was funded by the tobacco industry.

CHAPTER 2
The Voyage South

The ship, its horn echoing off the surrounding sheds, left the dock on time. Thrilled as he was, John had little time to stand at the rail to enjoy the departure; it was down to work immediately. The purser, in heavily accented English, pointed out the captain's salon to John and said, "There are 5 passengers and the captain to feed." He made it sound as if they were going to be eating from morning to night. "You'll be waiting on table; sweep up and set up." He soon learnt his duties also included housekeeping and bedmaking in the passengers' cabins.

Two of the passengers under his care were a doctor and his wife. They were fascinated by John's reason for going to Chile and were quick to realize that he needed some coaching in Spanish. They gave him two lessons a day during most of the voyage, teaching him enough to be comfortable with basic conversational Spanish. They loved hearing his life story and his skiing escapades; the Spanish lessons became a trade-off, one story for each lesson.

In return for *"donde esta la playa?"* John told them of the winter months spent camping in lean-to shelters on Tuckerman's Ravine high on Mt. Washington. He told of the terrifying shusses of Hillman's Highway and of the head-wall itself. Other lessons were traded for stories of escapades on Mt. Washington shared with Bruce Flemming, a jet test pilot with Canadair, Bud Keenan, Alex MacDougal, Peter Kingsmill and Bill Beck, all ardent skiers from Montreal, Ottawa and Toronto. His teachers were not winter-wise. They found it hard to imagine that people would endure a climb of one and a half hours, from the Pinkham Notch base to the snow slopes of Tuckerman, and then on skis, climb higher again on the precipitous slopes; all for the thrill of a single few minute's descent.

John still gets a laugh out of this particular lesson trade-off: "There's a restaurant at the base of Tuckerman's Ravine nicknamed Howard Johnsons. They used bottled propane for heating and cooking and we were asked to carry empty tanks down the mountain in exchange for a free supper. The empty tanks were known as "goofer bombs". The lesson that day included Spanish for "where is the bathroom?".

John worked diligently for three days. He quickly developed a good pair of sea legs which he attributed to his balance learned in skiing. Although the Atomena was rolling in swells larger than any John had seen on inland waters, he did not spill a single tray. On the fourth day at sea the Captain told him he would be kept on as a member of the crew. He was interested in John's mission and would have loved to see him in action in Chile. He sat with him from time to time and exchanged stories, John telling of canoe trips over white water, and the Captain, seafaring tales that excited John's imagination. He was surprised that this real man of adventure considered him to be an adventurer as well.

It seemed to John that the Captain listened to his stories enviously: the stories of many canoe trips from Maniwaki, in the north of the Gatineau system, trips as long as 7 days, filled with adventure, paddling down 31 Mile Lake, white-watering in the river rapids, portaging, camping amid the scenic solitude of the Gatineau valley. The Captain was astonished when John told him of the Rideau trip from Smiths Falls to Ottawa, sixty miles that he and his father had made in one day! He had heard of the voyageurs of Canada's past and he seemed to believe that he had one on his ship. Things were looking good; Chile was less than 7000 miles away.

After passing through the Panama Canal the Atomena arrived in Buena Ventura, the main seaport of Colombia, to off-load her cargo of truck chassis. This occupied the next ten days and John's education in seamanship and other worldly matters widened.

"What keeps a steel ship free of rust?" John wished he had never asked; in answer he was handed a bucket of blue paint and a large paint brush.

Between sessions of painting the vessel from stem to stern, and looking after his five passengers, John would high-dive off the Atomena's bridge as he used to dive off the cliffs of the Gatineau River with his brother Harvey. There was one difference – back home John could take his time swiming ashore after the dive if he felt so inclined. Here in Colombia, he got out of the murky water in a hurry, climbing back on board as fast as he possibly could. The stories of sharks lurking in the water were highly motivating.

On the occasional trip ashore with the ship's officers, he saw another side of life that was new to him; far removed from his way of life on the outskirts of Ottawa. He was shocked at the unsavory establishments that back home would be called houses of ill-repute.

The Atomena left Colombia with her holds empty and sailed on to Guyaquil, Ecuador, where she picked up a cargo of bananas. Streams of workmen, sweating in the tropical heat, carried huge bunches of bananas on board. They filled the holds to overflowing and then covered the decks with the unripened fruit. Every available nook had its cache of bananas. John had hardly seen a banana in his life; he tried a ripe one, and was delighted with it. For a dollar one of the labourers brought a bunch of over 200 bananas below deck to John's cabin. On that first day, he ate thirty-two. He pictured a continuous trail of banana skins floating in the ship's wake over the last three thousand miles of the journey.

Aside from the binding effect of too many bananas, the balance of the trip to Valparaiso was uneventful. John felt some regret as he descended the gangplank for the last time. The trip had been tough, but the ship and his shipmates of the past month had found a warm place in his heart. He felt good, he had a few dollars in his pocket and he was at long last in Chile. Heartwarming calls of "Good luck and see you soon!" came from the rails above him. John replied at the top of his voice, "See you in a few months!" With his kit bag on one shoulder and the ever-present ski boots slung over the other, he spun on his heel. With a straight back he walked away from the ship and off the pier.

Chapter 3
Chile

John had a letter of introduction from the C.A.S.A president, Mr. Sydney Dawes, to a Mr. Augustine Edwards who owned the prominent banking complex named the Edwards Bank. It was Mr. Edwards who had issued the invitation to Canada to participate in the 'Union of the Americas' Ski Meet. John pulled the letter from his pocket feeling that it was his only line to reality. The letter was vague. There was no mention of how to find Senor Edwards.*"Donde esta la banco?"* (Where is the bank?), in his newly-acquired Spanish eventually led John to an inconspicuous little corner bank. The bank's manager was very surprised and John had difficulty explaining why he was there. "No, I am not selling bananas. I know I came on a banana boat. Look, ski boots! Please, I must see Mr. Edwards." How he wished Mr. Dawes had written the introductory letter in Spanish! *"Senor Edwards, Senor Edwards, por favor."*

An interpreter of sorts was found and things became a little easier. John was informed, very graphically with flapping arms and diving hands, that Mr. Edwards was a hundred miles away in the City of Santiago, flying one of his fleet of seven aircraft. They said they would contact him immediately and in only 4 hours they had reached him. John would soon discover that this was fast by South American standards. On Edwards' instructions, the bank's manager took care of John's first night ashore.

Following his host's instructions to the letter, John arrived in the Santiago train station where he met Mr. Arturo Podesta, the president of the Chilean Ski Federation. Mr. Podesta welcomed him with open arms trying to hide the incredulous look on his face. The Chileans had invited all the western hemisphere countries to participate in this first-ever Pan American ski meet and were they surprised by the first arrival – a Canadian with his own boots and almost enough money in his pocket to buy a pair of skis and poles!

The red carpet was rolled out and John was about to find out what it was like to be treated as a visiting dignitary. The first Canadian to ski competitively in the Andes was, for the next few months, to be a guest with all expenses paid. All that remained for him to do was to sell the cigarettes he had brought with him to raise a few more dollars to purchase his equipment. The Camels sold quickly, doubling his investment.

He went to the one-and-only supplier of skis in Santiago and was disappointed to find that they were still using the 'old-fashioned' rubber super-diagonal heel binding. John had been using the recently-designed leather lanier strap binding, developed by the French team and used by Emile Allais, the world champion, himself. He took his newly-purchased Northland skis to a carpenter. Carefully, through a competent interpreter, he explained he wanted a mortise cut through the ski from one side to another under the heel, to accommodate the yards of leather lace that would bind his heels to the skis. His hosts could not believe that he was going to bind his foot solidly to the ski. They were also sure he would never make it all the way down the course on the weakened skis: "You want a hole drilled through your skis?" They could only imagine his hitting a bump on the treacherous course and shattering the ski into splinters. When John eventually saw the mountains and the terrain he was about to ski, he feared they might be right.

Then it was off to Portillo where the races were to be held. The train ride, complicated by a transfer, was a long, jolting, seven-hour journey. Passing through magnificent scenery; snow covered mountain passes, snow sheds and tunnels reminded John of the toy trains that tooted around department store windows at Christmas time. He was not pressing his face to the the store window looking in, he was on the toy train looking out.

John stepped off the train at Portillo into the winter wonderland that had been passing by the train's windows. The station was completely shadowed by the surrounding 17,000-foot snow-covered, sunlit peaks. The crisp dry snow with its promise of fantastic schussing lay all about. The musty, steamy air of the train was replaced by the cool dry air of the high Andes. He was back in his element.

The races were scheduled for the 15th of August, only 1 month away. There would hardly be enough time to acclimatize to the 9000 foot altitude and to get in shape.

The Chileans were concerned with what they considered to be a lack of snow.

With only 15 feet on the ground instead of the customary 35, they had cause to worry. Realizing that the only North American team to show up in time was Canada's, in the person of John Clifford, the Championships of the Western Hemisphere were cancelled. But all was not lost. All that was needed was more time, and there was plenty of that. In the hope that everything would improve, the meet was re-scheduled a month ahead to September 15, 1946, and the name was also changed to the 'Chilean Championships'. Chance had given John the time he needed.

He welcomed the change; another month of royal treatment suited him just fine. The additional training time was also going to prove invaluable.

Skiers from Bolivia, Peru, Argentina and Chile began to arrive and were billeted, along with John, in the Refugio, idyllically situated in the valley near the one slope that was served by a platter tow.

The Refugio, located about a half a mile from the ski area, could accommodate about a hundred skiers. It was like any fancy chalet at a major ski resort in North America. The commuting to and from the Refugio was accomplished in a unique vehicle known as "the gondola". In reality it was a converted gas-powered bus that travelled along a cog railway. It was suitable for transporting only 35 people at a time which caused a small traffic jam every morning and evening.

It was more than a month after leaving New York when John first set foot on his new skis. Portillo's 9000-foot altitude was taking some getting used to. He did not attempt to get up to his usual speed during training the first week. The other skiers, acclimatized to high-altitude skiing, watched him arrive breathless at the finish line after running a few gates, thinking Canada would be a pushover. But John, too, was watching.

After one week of acclimatization and a little skiing, John was beginning to feel more at home. As breathing got easier he was able to accelerate his training pace and his downhill speed. The practise hill had the one and only ski tow in use. It was a home made platter-pull affair about 2500 feet long with a vertical rise of only 400 feet. Ski tows and lifts were a relatively new feature of the sport; they were to play an important part in John Clifford's future.

The week spent skiing on this slope was a real education: "The only thing that felt familiar to me was the hill and the snow, a four or five hundred foot vertical over 2500 feet was just like home once you got used to the altitude. The different techniques of the other skiers, and trying to communicate with them, well that was another story. We used sign language and a lot of body english that everyone seemed to understand. With our swooping arms and dancing hips we looked like a cross between a conga line and a squadron of fighters. We all loved skiing with a passion, we wanted to pass on tips to each other, but there was always the undercurrent of knowing that you didn't want to tell all because you'd be racing this guy in a few days on a mountain a hell of a lot bigger than this one. I admit those guys were good, but were they good enough to beat me? Was I good enough to beat them? I wasn't sure . . . their high mountain experience might be my downfall."

As the week wore on, John felt his lack of high mountain exposure was the only element that might keep him from winning. He knew that he was faster than his fellow competitors, but he had to get away from them and the lower slopes. He really wanted to open up, as he had not skied to his potential since arriving at Portillo. He had to ski the high country, he had to get used to the very thin air up on the "Roca Jack" where the race would be run, and he had to do it soon just to keep his confidence up. Skiers were not allowed to climb the steep slopes unaccompanied; how could he ski it without revealing his potential to his competitors? He was alone and now he found himself wishing that George was still with him. Enviously he watched the others head up to higher altitudes in teams, team-mates helping each other.

When he was just about to give up asking for permission to ski the higher mountains alone, South Americas prestigious guest, the world's fastest skier and current world champion, France's Emile Allais arrived on the scene. The father of the revolutionary French technique and the long-thong lanier binding that John alone was using, was to be the race's forerunner.

Emile had an obligation to ski the high country with the Chilean team members and, after meeting John, he insisted that he ski with them. He spent long days skiing on the vast sweeping powder snow fields with top Chilean racers Chaco Dominguez, Tito Belledonne, Nano Oelckers, J. Errazuriz and Arturo Hammersley, the latter a former instructor at Snow Valley in the US. John's new friends were skiing with complete abandon. He could feel his body taking on new strength and his technique, with each descent, gained a new degree of proficiency. It was a glorious, unforgettable time in the young skier's life. It was fun and he had to work hard at remembering the real reason he was there... to win the big race. The joy of skiing the spectacular South American mountains was fine but following Emile Allais and trying to emulate his every move was more important.

After a few days on the mountain Emile noticed that John was always in his shadow. He recognized the young Canadian's potential, and to John's delight, he decided to unleash himself and ski with the daring and assurance for which he was famous. If the Canadian or the others could keep up, *et bien*. If not, so be it!

John now thought, "If I can keep up with this man I may just have a chance of winning." Emile Allais knew that he had a willing and apt pupil in his companion and John was learning what world class skiing was all about. The two became daily ski mates. Skiing behind Allais on the great Andean runs was a close-up of the best. Allais' speed and daring proved to be too much for most of the others, but John, determined to copy the master, blasted on behind, grimly set on seeing each run through just as the renowned racer had taken it. Here was training to bring out the best in any racer!

Three weeks of this: skiing all day and then evening discussions with his mentor about strategy and technique. As John and the French star had no common language the sessions were very animated. "Emile would point to the position of a knee or foot. I would copy him, he would smile or shake his head." John was skiing better than ever before in his life.

Both men had underlying motives in mind when they became friends and started to ski together. Allais had just accepted the position of head coach for the Canadian Olympic team that was being put together for the '48 Olympic games and John was the first Canadian skier that he had met. When John learned of that fact, he not only wanted to win the Chilean Championship, he wanted to be a member of the Canadian Olympic team.

The championships loomed. The course, a two mile killer with a 3,000 foot drop, had to be mastered. Wisely Emile had saved the best for the last. He asked John if he was ready for the ultimate run. The next day was to be their introduction to the Roca Jack.

CHAPTER 4

The Race

"Roca Jack day" dawned clear and bright. John and Emile were on the mountain before the first light touched the snow-fields. The climbing became a little less fatiguing as the sun rose higher over the mountains, imperceptibly warming the snow's surface. The snow, with its fine untouched crust surface, accepted their skis with less backslip as they switchbacked towards the powdery summit and the start of the Roca Jack run. Shadows from the surrounding peaks shaded the area as they climbed higher and higher. Their skis were enveloped by weightless dry powder as they neared the summit, promising them a downhill run bordering on perfection.

The Roca Jack was an incredible sight. It was, as he had feared, bigger skiing than he had yet experienced. John had heard that the first section of the course was a straight schuss, a drop of 1500 feet. They had told him that it was easy to hit 80 miles an hour if you were able to keep on your feet. At first he had doubted the stories of these high speeds: now as he looked down the run he was fast becoming a believer. And he could only see the top half of the run. Emile reminded him that after the curve, barely discernable in the distance far below, the course dropped another blindingly fast 1500 feet into the valley towards the finish line in the village of Los Andes.

Allais thrust with his poles and was gone in a flash. The flying powder behind the speeding skier was a sight to behold. John stood mesmerized as Emile disappeared in a dazzling display of speed and form around the bend into the lower section.

John was standing in awe when he remembered that it was now his turn. He pushed off as if into the jaws of hell; today he admits that he was never so scared in his life. "I felt the rush of the thin air as my speed was building up, my skis wanted to fly. Concentrating on staying in the thin track Emile had left behind I became unconscious of my speed. Was I going as fast as Emile? There was no way to tell. I crouched even lower as I entered the turn that I knew marked the half way point. My legs were starting to feel the strain of the long upper schuss, another mile to go . . . should I stand higher to slow up a little or go for it? No, a champion would never slow up. I crouched even lower, expecting to crash at any time. Miliseconds later I christied to a stop in the area where the finish line would be. I'll never forget it- Emile rushed over to me and told me in his broken English that unless I learned to slow up I would not live to be a champion." John had passed his first world class test but, through watching Emile's descent, he knew he still had a lot to learn. With the competition only days away John's solitary fear was . . . would he be as good as he wanted to be?

September skiing in Chile, being late in the season, meant spring-like conditions. Schussing Roca Jack every day under snow conditions that varied from powder at the top, to corn mid-way, and then to packed or icy at the bottom built up John's skill and strength. His knees were no longer shaking at the end of a training run and with Emile's watchful eye and coaching his technique had vastly improved. At this point Emile's only concern was whether John could stand up to the strain of world class competition on race day.

Skiing at 70 to 80 miles an hour became for John like a walk in the park. He was all confidence, then: "My skis were running at top speed in the narrow track of a previous run; I was schussing straight down when I must have momentarily lost my concentration; my left ski climbed out of the packed track and caught powder. The eggbeater that followed was the worst fall I'd ever had. My knee hurt like hell and I was sure it was all over."

The pain in his knee was diagnosed as pulled ligaments and he was prescribed rest until the race, just a few days away. His hosts thought that this was a good idea since a pre-race party was to be held in Santiago; a good rest with a little partying thrown in would be just what the doctor ordered. John would have preferred to continue his skiing but gave way to pain and social pressure.

Race day weather was perfect and John's knee appeared to have repaired itself. He drew the fifth starting position for a race that was to be held under perfect snow conditions. There had been a fresh fall of snow overnight and the course had been packed by soldiers tramping up and down on foot. The conditions were absolutely made to order for John; he was sure to win . . . if only his untried knee did not giveout.

CANADIAN
Sport MONTHLY

THE NATIONAL SKI Magazine WITH ALL CLASS SPORTS IN SEASON

DECEMBER, 1946   "THE MAGAZINE DEVOTED TO NATIONAL FITNESS"   Vol. XXXIII No. 8

Read the remarkable story of a young Canadian who travelled on his own for 16,000 miles to win a major ski championship and act as goodwill ambassador extraordinary in South America.

"John Clifford, Chile Champ". Appearing January Issue.

JOHN CLIFFORD OF OTTAWA WINNER OF THE 1946 CHILE COMBINED CHAMPIONSHIP
Seen in a fast and tricky turn, blond John Clifford, for two years captain of the Ottawa Ski Club's famous Night Riders, worked his way to Chile this summer, won the national championships at Portillo, Chile, and the hearts of South American skiers with a thrilling display. Seen again at left wearing No. 6 he is photographed with world champion, Emile Allais, famous French Ski School head who will teach this winter at Valcartier, near Quebec.

Allais fore-ran the course, and the race was on. There were some forty top skiers, the cream of Argentina, Bolivia, and Chile. The three Chileans who preceded him fell on the course and were injured. Waiting for his turn, John was undergoing another new experience; he was getting psyched out, losing confidence. Would he fall? Would his knee take the strain? Being a one-man team, he did not have moral support at that crucial moment. Fortunately, having drawn the fifth starting position, he didn't have long to wait before he was on the course.

They called it a suicide run. He blasted into the course; the familiar downhill rush was upon him . . . the straight schuss into the turn . . . and then disaster; he fell at the first control gate. He regained his feet as soon as he hit the packed snow, traversed to the next gate in his best cross-country style. From there on, with a picture of Allais in his mind, he let gravity take full hold. Down low, into his crouch, no doubts now . . . staying low . . . going for it!

His fears proved to be unfounded. The taped knee did not let him down. His newly-acquired high-speed "French" technique, his weeks of practice, and his determination to win came through. Flashing across the finish line, he knew that he had done well.

Even with the fall, John won the first Chilean Winter Games downhill. He beat the famous Oelckers by a full 16 seconds and was only eight seconds behind Allais . . . an unofficial 2:13 for the French Champion; 2:21 for John; while second place Oelckers was back at 2:37. He was elated with the win. With the Roca Jack downhill behind him he was not worried about the next day's slalom race.

John and his Chilean
trophies, 1946.

The slalom, set by Edwards and Allais, was a two-run combined time competition against formidable competition. John skied a conservative first run; he had to do much better on the second to stay in competition. Once again, skill and fortitude paid off; on the second trip through the gates he put together the fastest run of the day.

His combined time, less than half a second behind the winner, gave him second place in the slalom competition. However, the meet was his. His combined time for both events, downhill and slalom, gave him the overall win. John was the fastest skier in the western hemisphere. He was sure a place on Canada's Olympic team was in the bag. Ominously, the media at home hardly noticed.

Not so in South America. His triumph was as popular as if he were a native son. He received seven trophies at the prize-giving ceremony; other competitors gave him everything from pins and sweaters to a new pair of European-made skis. The celebration that night at Refugio saw the dawn.

A few days later, promising to return, John said goodbye to his companions and hosts at Portillo and headed back to Santiago. Once again, red carpet treatment; he enjoyed the hospitality of friends for the next month. The ski fraternity never seemed to tire of entertaining their new national champion. Nightly wining and dining and daily visits to race tracks and casinos filled the time.

Mercifully, the Atomena returned to Chile, and he signed on for the homeward voyage. On this journey, the ship had no passengers to be cared for, so John was taken on as a seaman. Sea-legs for ski-legs: a fair trade for passage home.

CHAPTER 5
The Voyage Home

Feeling very much at home, John boarded the ship a few weeks prior to her departure. "I was given the same paint brush that had become so much a part of me on the way down; I felt I was being reunited with an old friend." Yesterday's hero was now just an ordinary sailor, doing what sailors do all over the world while waiting to take to the sea. The term "from stem to stern" took on real meaning as he replaced ski pants with bell bottoms and traded the skipole for a paint brush.

John's ten shipmates were a far different lot than those of his first voyage; they were a very earthy bunch. The trip up the west coast of South America was uneventful. John was assigned to the bridge where he would steer the ship for two hours on watch and two hours off around the clock. The boredom of the dark duty hours was broken by daylight sightings of porpoise and whales. The days were very long. Gone were the inspirational conversations and Spanish lessons of the southbound voyage. In fact, there was very little conversation at all. Only one of his shipmates, a Norwegian, could speak any English. He was an interesting if somewhat unsavoury character. John made the best of this man's company, but there was no real affinity.

When the Atomena was tied up in Valparaiso, a cargo of wine in barrels was taken on. At sea, the crew broke into the precious cargo; the tasting became a drunken orgy and in short order, they were unable to function. Fights broke out, heads were smashed, arms and legs were broken. John avoided it all by remaining on duty and not volunteering to help break up the party. With the crew locked away in the ship's brig, the Captain, with John's help, brought the Atomena into the harbour of Arica, in northern Chile, but not without incident. At the entrance to the harbour the ship struck a large piece of flotsam, damaging its screw seriously enough to require immediate repairs.

The ship remained in port for the next ten days awaiting a navy tug boat to tow it back to a Valparaiso dry dock for repairs. The few days in Arica proved to be a great temptation to the crew, and when it was time to leave, only John and his Norwegian friend reported. Since the ship was being towed by a Chilean navy tug, and Valperaiso was no more than two days away, the Captain was satisfied with the size of his crew.

Back to the monotony of chipping and painting. A full month later, repairs completed, they once again set sail. Now lonely and homesick, John was eager to get on with the voyage.

Stripping the rust and old paint was not the only sort of stripping that John's Norse shipmate proved capable of. With the Captain occupied in the various ports of call on the way to Cuba, this character proceeded to strip the ship of anything he could sell. Any small boat that came alongside was a potential customer. He sold milk, butter, eggs, meat; he had sold off much of the ships' cutlery when he had the audacity to break into the Captain's liquor supply and sold some of that.

"We were in the port of Balboa on our way through the Panama Canal, hanging over the side on a scaffold doing our usual scraping and painting, when a small boat came alongside. In Spanish, the man on board asked if it would be possible to buy some rope. My shipmate told him to return at the same time the next day. I don't know how he did it, but when the customer returned he was passed the end of a 2000 foot bail of 1 inch manilla rope through a porthole near the waterline. The rope sank below the surface and it was pulled unseen to the far side of another vessel anchored nearby. After this, even though I was afraid of what the man might do to me, I informed the Mate and the Captain." The man was watched but not detained, as the Captain had other plans for him.

Departing Balboa, the Atomena passed through the Panama Canal and headed to Havana, docking there with some material shortage, but without incident. The ship would be in port awaiting loading for ten days. Although short-handed the captain allowed the crew, including the Norwegian, a few days ashore. "The second mate and I had become good friends and together we did a lot of sight-seeing in Havana. This was during Batista's time and the contrast of wealth and poverty was very evident. You could see that you either had it or you didn't; you were either rich or poor."

John had never seen anything like it before; the Cubans either lived in shacks and makeshift hovels, or in mansions; there was no apparent middle class. There was a shortage of food for the mass and an overabundant larder for the few. John was forever affected by his Cuban experience. Poverty existed in South America too, but there he had been shielded from its stark reality by the relatively wealthy company he had kept. He had briefly experienced the life at the top and was now a witness to existence at the bottom. He was not certain what he wanted out of life beyond being an Olympic skier, but he now knew what he didn't want.

At departure time, only four showed up: the Captain, the second mate, the engineer and John. The Norwegian was, as the captain had expected, among the missing. "On the Captain's orders we searched all the bars, local seamens' haunts and brothels and, as predicted, we found our man. He was arrested and brought back to the ship where he was locked up for the return trip to New York where he was to be turned over to the authorities. I now understood the Captain's thinking when he let that crook free to traipse about in Havana. Knowing his man, he knew that he would not roam far from Havana's red light district. Why bother with him until it was time to leave ...he knew he would be able to find him when the time came."

The Atomena left Havana scheduled to arrive in New York on December 6, 1946. Being short-handed seemed to be no problem. She sailed up the US coastline with ease and dignity. John was becoming quite proud of his well painted vessel.

As they proceeded northward the temperature steadily dropped. The wind rose to gale force. The last day at sea, somewhere north of Cape Hatteras, was the most frightening experience of the whole journey; a winter storm on a severely short-handed ship.

The gale struck with ferocious intensity. Wave after wave broke over the ship leaving a fresh layer of ice each time. The buildup of ice on the deck was so thick that John believed that she'd roll over. And she might have if they had remained at sea any longer, but they entered calmer waters as they neared New York. To John the waves seemed as high as the Andes that he had just skied.

"I couldn't believe it when the Captain told me to leave the ship's wheel to go forward to the spindle to drop anchor. When he saw me hesitate, the Captain said that anyone who could ski down the highest mountain in the Andes could surely negotiate an ice-laden deck. I reminded him that it was only I that moved on the mountain; the mountain stood still.

"I put on every piece of clothing I had except my ski boots, and made my way forward asking myself what Allais would say if he could see me now" It took all of his considerable strength and balance to negotiate the heaving deck. Walls of freezing spray engulfed him with each downward pitch of the ship. When he reached the spindle he was a walking man of ice. His clothing was so encrusted that he had to smash his arm against a stanchion to break it free.

He was barely able to bend his arms when the command to drop anchor was signalled above the roaring wind. He activated the mechanism, grabbed hold of a support, and clung there freezing, until the ship heaved to a full stop.

CHAPTER 6
Nature's Child

John Clifford was born, along with his twin sister Florence, on February 13, 1923 in Ottawa, Ontario. His mother Mary and father Fred were a hard-working couple of modest means. He was the first born son and the eldest (by seconds) of four children. Although his family lived through tough times in the early years of his childhood, he felt secure; in fact, favoured.

In 1924, when John was only two years old, the family moved to a 200 acre farm in an idyllic setting in Oakpoint, New Brunswick, 30 miles up the St. John river from the city of the same name.

The farm had potential, but after four years of hard labour, Clifford senior was not satisfiued with the results and once again John and family were on the train, heading back to Ottawa.

John was too young to have done much more than pick dandelions on the farm. The only incident he remembers of those days was of Father and family driving the thirty miles to St. John by horse and buggy.

Back in Ottawa, Fred rented a ten-acre farm on Riverside Drive. The Clifford family by this time had grown to include brothers Bob and Harvey, one cow and some chickens.

Fred Clifford took on the job of driving a bread wagon, leaving mother Mary to some of the farming chores and the raising of John, brothers and sister.

During the bread wagon year, Fred Clifford also studied for and wrote the exams for the customs an excise department of the Canadian government. Two jobs and studies allowed only a few hours sleep per night. He persevered and passed the exam. For a man who had arrived from Liverpool when he was only ten this was a demonstration of perseverance and tenacity that John was to emulate throughout his life.

The first school that John attended was in Mooney's Bay. Bayview, a one-room school, was a three mile round trip from home that he and twin sister Florence walked each day. One afternoon before setting out on the homeward trek, John was playing tag with a few classmates when he ran in front of some older boys playing baseball. He was struck unconscious by a violent blow on the head with the bat. He was rushed to the hospital where his parents spent an anxious four hours awaiting his return to consciousness. As a result of this accident, John was to suffer an almost total loss of sight in his right eye and short-sightedness in his left. Many years of therapy helped very little, in fact, so little that the doctors upon further examination concluded that part of his vision problem was inherited. John would have to go through life with severely impaired eyesight.

Another move took place in 1932 when the new family house that John's father had been building was completed. The house, located on 34 Glendale Avenue in Ottawa, was near Glebe Collegiate, making it the high school of choice for John. John was a poor student at Glebe until half-way through grade ten when he rebelled against the courses he was taking. Latin was not his forte, and when he received a 6% mark on a mid-term paper he decided to change to the Ottawa Technical School and he began to get excellent results in maths, shops, and printing, subjects he felt could be of of real worth to him in the future.

Fred Clifford was an ardent outdoorsman. He enjoyed swimming and canoeing in the summer and cross-country skiing in the winter. He would not let his son John become a recluse, hiding behind his handicap. Poor eyesight and all, John had to perform. Under his father's guidance, he soon learned to love canoeing and camping. At about this time, John was introduced to his first pair of skis; barrel staves with strips of rubber for bindings. The first hill . . . the creek bank out in back of the house.

John, Florence, Harvey and Bob, around 1936.

Other than a brief stint as choir and altar boy with the St. Matthews church, religion played only a small part in John's upbringing. "Actually religion paid my way to my first temptation of any consequence. St. Matthews paid me fifteen cents a week. Ten cents was enough for a movie on Saturday afternoon, leaving 5 cents over; enough for a package of Turret cigarettes. I started smoking and didn't give it up 'til 30 years later." Cubs and then Boy Scouts were another enthusiasm during his pre-teen and teen age years. He enjoyed two weeks each summer camping with the Scouts at MacClaren's Landing. John's leadership training under scoutmaster Fred Sharp was another plus in his formative years. He was by nature on the quiet side, if not a little shy. His scouting experience, as a patrol leader helped draw him out of his shell.

Summer camping did not end with the two weeks at scout camp. Fred loved to go weekend canoe camping, taking the whole Clifford family along. Sons John, Bob and the younger Harvey became efficient paddlers and the sport rubbed off on them. Every summer throughout their teens the brothers were seldom at home. The call of the surrounding rivers was irresistible, and the boys, like their father, were out on the water.

In December of 1939, John decided that he had had enough of formal schooling and tried to enlist in the armed services. He was turned down because of his poor eyesight, but he was offered a position as office boy and printer with the RCAF at their Headquarters in Ottawa.

He had five happy, profitable years, working for the Government, during which time he formed a pleasant working relationship with his immediate superior Mr. Herb Rushleau. Mr. Rushleau was an energenic, encouraging man, the kind of boss that any young man should have on his first job, and perhaps, in future, to emulate.

The war curtailed most organised competitive sports, but John did play a little football with Ottawa's Winged Wheelers. Brother Harvey, who became Head Boy at Glebe Collegiate, stayed competitive by playing high school hockey. Skiing, however, was the sport of choice for both boys. Afternoons and evenings saw the brothers and sister Florence heading cross-country over Dows Lake, some four miles to the Experimental Farm. "We built jumps on narrow trails through the bush to increase our fun. Our skis were equipped with Higgin Bindings and Super Diagonals, allowing us to run cross-country and, with the diagonals solidly fastening our heels down, we were able to manage the downhills pretty effectively."

The OSC year book of 1943-44 that reported John's placing in the combined event also reported the results of the Interscholastic Girls Combined Downhill and Slalom. The winning team from Glebe Collegiate, represented by one Margaret Phillips, was presented with the Mrs. Robert E. Maynard Trophy.

Fred Clifford, centre, with his skiing family: John, Bob, Florence and Harvey.

Skiing was very much a family affair for the Cliffords, mostly centered about the Ottawa Ski Club. Sister Florence and brother Harvey also carried the family banner in the 43-44 yearbook. The Clifford name can be found in many club yearbooks to follow, though not always linked with racing. Florence, it was noted in one issue, "was a girl able to make the long round trip with 6 male escorts." Fred Clifford is also mentioned many times for his carpentry contributions. Off-season reports frequently told of trail cutting and bridge building involving Fred and his sons.

Winters melted into spring and summer. The frozen lakes and rivers were barely open before John was out on the water. In the summer of 1945, he took up serious rowing at the Ottawa Rowing Club. His competitive drive came forth on the water as on snow; he liked winning.

The Night Riders were started by Joe Morin in 1919 to clear and maintain the cross-country trails at Camp Fortune. George Brittain took over as captain in 1933, followed by Bill Irving in 1939 and John Clifford in 1948.

John may have been a little shy in a social context but not when it came to extolling the virtues of his favourite sports; evenings in the Night Riders' bunkhouse were always enlivened by John's stories of canoe trips and paddling competitions of preceding summers.

One of those winter evenings when the trail clearing was done and supper was

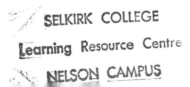

behind them, he persuaded fellow Night Riders Jim Bisson and Gabby Beaudry to join the rowing club with him. They all became ardent rowers. Weather permitting, they rowed every day, striving to be the club's best.

The Night Riders of Camp Fortune were to leave their mark in the Ottawa Rowing Club's record book. One regatta in particular, against the Brockville Rowing Club, is well worth noting: John, weighing only 145 pounds, stroked the light fours and the light eights as well as the heavy fours and the heavy eights, winning 4 out of 11 races. John and his friends did well at other regattas against Montreal teams, the Rideau Canoe Club and the Carleton Place Club. Gabby Beaudry went on to become a Canadian Singles Sculling Champion.

The independence he had learned as an individual downhill racer, racing against the clock, did not handicap John as a member of a racing shell's crew; he was a committed team player as well. His fellow crew members remember his constant desire to get the team out on the river to practise and then to practise again. "Too bad ski racing couldn't be man on man," he would often say to himself, as he raced another boat to the finish line.

John did not let his night work in construction interfere with his daytime sports activities. The seasons continued to run one into

Night Riders Headquarters: Rear: Harvey Clifford, John Clifford, Ken Thomas, Elmer Cassell, Clarence Fuller. Front: Walter Roach, Stew Parsons, Ted Grant, Bill Irving, Fred Richardson, Fred Hanna, George Brittain.

Night Riders, lunch break.

Night Riders at Plaunt Lodge: Rear: Gordy Grant, Alex Hussey.
Front: Ted Crain, Fred Foster, Bill Tindale, John Buck,
Ron Baillie, Ken Mielke, Dalton Wood.

the other. At the Edinburgh Canoe Club in 1948 he was introduced to water skiing, the summer version of snow skiing, then in its infancy.

John and a friend, Bernie Garand, a fellow member of the canoe club, decided that it was time to try the fledgling sport. They couldn't find a pair of skis to borrow, and so John, with his native ingenuity, came up with an answer. He nailed wide strips of masonite onto an old pair of snow skis, and added a binding made from an old tire tube. The only craft that was available was a ten-foot rowboat with a tired ten-horsepower outboard motor. The Ottawa River never saw a more pitiful attempt at water skiing; needless to say they had great difficulty . . . but they did waterski and they loved it!

Deciding there was potential in the new sport, John bought a pair of Pierre Beaudin Sea Gliders from Morgan's Department Store in Montreal. He arranged for the use of a more powerful tow boat, and taught himself to water ski in just a few days.

CHAPTER 7
Summer and Winter

Both John and Harvey would find it difficult to say which they preferred, summer with its canoe trips or winter and its skiing. "We were skiing at The Ottawa Ski Club's Camp Fortune when Mr. C.E. Mortureaux, the president, persuaded us to join the Ottawa and Edinburgh Canoe Club in 1940. He was president of the canoe club as well and he was very convincing. He described the river trip from Maniwaki in the far north back to the club house in Ottawa. He told us of taking the train up to Maniwaki and of the seven heavenly days of white-watering and camping on rivers leading to 31 Mile, Pemichangan and Big Whitefish lakes, and on into the Lievre River. We didn't need much convincing. Harvey and I joined the club, learned to be competitive paddlers and rowers...and we made the Maniwaki trip three times over the next three years. My brother and I fell passionately in love with the Gatineau valley." John enjoyed those trips, as he said, "with a passion," and he had his first glimpse of the majestic Mont St. Marie.

In the summer of 1945 Harvey Clifford, enjoying the thrill of high-diving into the rushing waters of Devil's Hole at Hogsback on the Rideau River, was spotted by Mr. Philip Jenner, an English filmmaker. Mr Jenner was visiting Ottawa and, like any tourist, he had his camera slung about his neck. The photo session of Harvey diving into the scenic river led to tales of the north country, of the lakes, rivers and streams not far away. The boys' love of the wilderness was obvious. Mr Jenner asked if there were any cliffs that they might dive from, and if so, would they put together a trip at once. Quick negotiations led to a seven day all expenses paid trip to Maniwaki, a trip they would have gladly made for nothing!

Harvey, John and two other paddling buddies, Phil Bott and Pat Sligh, gathered up the necessary supplies and equipment and were on the train the next day with their benefactor. The young men showed him some of the most beautiful scenery that Canada had to offer. John and Harvey guided the canoe party down the Gatineau and across 31 Mile Lake onto the Lievre river. Wherever they found high cliffs, some more than a hundred feet high, the expedition would stop for a photo session, the boys diving repeatedly from the clifftops.

At one point in the trip, after a long and difficult portage from Lake Pemichangan to Bagnal lake, John and his party met Denise Colson, and her three daughters, Marianne, Deedee and Jane. They camped that night in front of her house on nearby lake Oxbow. Mrs. Colson was happy to have male company that night as, just the night before, a black bear had visited their camp. She showed them the deep claw marks on her back door. The "heroes", armed with a .22 caliber rifle borrowed from Mrs. Colson, assured the ladies of their safety and prepared to bed down for the night.

The sun had just set when a pair of bears appeared. A noisy welcome of shouting and gunfire sent the bears packing. Mr. Jenner, camera in hand, prayed that there was enough light for the pictures he had taken. His Canadian adventure was a little more than he had bargained for!

True to his word, Jenner took care of all expenses when they arrived back in Ottawa. With a promise to send them pictures, he departed, never to be seen or heard from again. Six years later, Deedee Colson was John's partner in a waterski doubles competition.

The end of World War II meant John could leave his wartime work to pursue his future in the real world. He had heard that a garage owner from Piedmont, Quebec, Guy Debassecourt, and Wilf Harris, the owner of the Wakefield Inn, in the town of the same name, were about to build a rope tow. Guy Debassecourt had built the first rope tow in St. Sauveur, Quebec, and, wishing to learn more from the expert, John offered his services. They could not refuse the energetic young man's request to work with them. He began by hand drilling and blasting out the tow's right-of-way. This completed, he helped erect poles and pulleys, and rigging of rope to the old truck chassis that was to power the tow. The experience was his higher education. Perhaps, John pondered, "this may be a way to make a living; outside enjoying nature, and developing the sport I love."

Winter weekends were spent at the Ottawa Ski Club where John was a member of the Night Riders, the group of volunteers responsible for clearing and maintaining the club's miles of cross-country trails and slalom hills. The young men who

Right: Night Riders at work: Steve Saunders, Peter Guy, Bob Gratton, John Clifford, Gordon Dean.
Below: 1945: the original rope tow, slalom hill, Camp Fortune.

performed these back-breaking chores in good weather and bad were a very dedicated bunch. In return for the hours spent in toil, the club gave the Night Riders free skiing and a free bunk for the weekend. John took full advantage of the offer. In their spare time, the Night Riders were encouraged to learn how to race for the club. He was developing his downhill and slalom skills as well as the cross-country abilities for which he had already received considerable acclaim. He would in return bring many accolades to the club as a competitor.

The winter of 1945-46 was the most important, perhaps the most influential year of John's life to date. His many hours spent working at Camp Fortune as a volunteer

Night Riders, building a bridge for a cross-country trail; John Clifford with hammer, front left.

Night Rider were about to blossom into a lifetime career in the ski industry. When Bill Irving, the Rider captain, and Fred Dixon asked him to help them run the canteen at Camp Fortune, fondly known as the slop shop, he accepted. It was a small step towards the ski tow installation and operating concession for the OSC that followed. With his foot in the door, he negotiated a five year concession agreement with the OSC to build and operate tows at Camp Fortune

The first tow that John built was a masterpiece of ingenuity and spare parts. It was not the first tow to be installed at Camp Fortune; one was built in 1942, on the club's Slalom Hill, by John P. Taylor, Hubert Douglas and John Carscadden. It was John's first rope-tow as well as his entry into the world of banking and "high finance". He did not have the necessary funds but thanks to Percy Woods, father of his friend Dalton, he was able to borrow $500 to get the job underway. "My father couldn't help me financially, but he did all the carpentry work, including building the tow shack housing the Packard motor we converted to drive the rope." Many years went by before John was able to repay the borrowed $500. But Mort's Hill and Camp Fortune had its second rope tow.

This tow made the ascent of the slalom hill faster and easier than ever before. Some of the hard-liners in the club considered a tow unnecessary. John disagreed. He wore out many a pair of thick horsehide gloves in his constant trying and testing. His skiing didn't suffer during this year of tow skiing; he continued his quest for more runs and more speed, and each test ride up on the tow meant another run down. Foremost in his skiing life was the desire to better his technique, to compete and to win.

He had been competing throughout his teenage years at every organized meet that the OSC held. Although the first published record of a John Clifford win is his second place in the Gatineau Ski Zone Senior Combined Downhill and Slalom Journal Trophy Race, held on March 14th 1943, and another second place on April 4th, this time beaten by brother Harvey by a tick of the clock, there were many prior, unpublished club wins. Flying down a mountain slope on winged skis under perfect control was the ultimate experience for this young man. Nevertheless, the more he skied, the more fascinated he became with the business end of skiing and, especially, uphill transportation.

CHAPTER 8
Return to Portillo

On John's return from Chile, on December 16, 1946, the St. Moritz winter Olympics were still two years in the future. As far as he was concerned, two years might as well have been a century. He was in the best physical and mental shape that he had ever been in and he knew that if the Olympic team were called together right then, he would be able to beat the best.

Winter had already arrived when he got off the bus at Ottawa's downtown terminal. No snow had been visible in the countryside on the northward drive, but it was cold. The disturbing thought of a delay in getting back to skiing was quickly dispelled by the inches of freshly fallen snow blanketing the city streets. He stopped on his long walk home to watch the noisy trucks, plows and snowblowers clearing the streets as if he had never seen such an operation before. Snow once again underfoot, he could hardly wait for morning to come, when he would be back at Camp Fortune, and back on skis.

After a fitful night's sleep, he arrived at Camp Fortune to find, due to his late return, that Bill Irving and Fred Dixon had completed the preparation of the hills and rope tows for the coming season. Everything was ready to go. It was only the 16th of December, and Fortune's 1946 ski season, a few weeks earlier than usual, was underway.

The Gatineau area received a generous snowfall that winter, a mixed blessing for John. More snow meant more skiers enjoying the club's facilities. More skiers... more work in maintaining the hills and trails to the high standard he had set. The many miles of cross-country trails, although still very well used, were losing devotees to the tows of the downhill and slalom slopes. Members wanted more uphill transportation, making it necessary for John to spend much of that winter building rope tows, leaving little time for training and even less for competition. His skiing may have suffered a little by this lack of training, but at the club level it was not noticeable; he repeatedly finished either first or second in any race that he found time to enter. His confidence never faltered, but he knew that the hills of Camp Fortune were not the mountains of Switzerland and he longed for international competition. Though he wanted to get away and ski the high country, he devotedly stuck to his obligation to the Ottawa Ski Club.

In the winter of 1947, the Canadian championships were held at Mont Ste. Anne near Quebec city. John arranged to leave his work at Fortune to participate. A place on the 1948 Olympic team was still uppermost in his mind; he considered that winning the championship would solidly nail down his Olympic chances. In order to be considered for the team, although he had done Canada proud in South America, he needed more recognition.

The media had not given him much publicity about his South American achievement. He was still an unknown because of his absence from major world class competition. Doing well at the club and provincial level since his return from Chile would not be enough to earn him the right to ski again for Canada. He needed a big win at home, and the publicity that would follow, to earn a place on the team.

He placed second to Pierre Jalbert. His time was respectably close, but he did not win! Swallowing his disappointment, he kept faith that his overall ability would get him the call to go to St. Moritz in February of 1948.

But the invitation did not come. As each member was chosen, John became more and more convinced that he was being overlooked. His brother Harvey was called, and others with whom he had skied, raced and beaten, were also invited to join the team. Was his second-place to Jalbert not good enough? Disappointed as he was, he decided he would train hard in the intervening time, preparing for the call-up that he still hoped would come. Eventually, he was asked to join the team as a spare, an alternate.

John's friend Emile Allais, as expected, was named coach of Canada's ski team. When spring training sessions started at Mont Tremblant in April, the old friendship was renewed. Emile reminded him that the final team was never chosen until the last minute, and if he continued to perform well, he could still be selected.

The snow left the Gatineau hills almost as fast as it had come, closing the facilities at Camp Fortune a few weeks early. Within hours of closing down the tows he gathered together his well-worn camping gear and was on the way to New

Hampshire's Mount Washington. Skiing the famous Tuckerman's Ravine, the treacherous Headwall and Hillman's Highway, on the highest mountain in the east, would help him catch up on the real mountain skiing that Camp Fortune could not provide.

Wooden lean-to shelters located near the summit of the mountain were a little more comfortable than sleeping under canvas. These shelters, provided by the New Hampshire mountaineering club, were not designed for winter use, but with some modifications, including hanging old blankets to help close the open side of the structure, they were quite comfortable even when the night-time temperature dipped well below zero.

John lived and skiied the mountain for more than a month with a few other hardy skiers. The cameraderie, sharing the hardships of winter camping and the thrill of climbing and skiing together, soon made fast friends of them all. Among them was his old friend Bruce Flemming, from Montreal, who was there on weekends only.

"There was a cabin restaurant in the camping area that was nicknamed Howard Johnson's. It was operated by an amiable man named Gus. Knowing the hardships of winter camping, he often helped the "permanent" residents of his mountaintop survive, providing occasional creature comforts, like canned goods left behind by weekend "tourists" or, in return for odd jobs, a hot meal. One night Bruce, who had somehow got hold of a can of white paint, decided to immortalize Gus for being such a nice guy. On a warm Saturday afternoon, he lowered himself on a rope half-way down a cliff-face high up on the mountain. Risking life and limb, he painted the name GUS in letters ten feet high across the cliff. Needless to say, when the Park Warden, Joe Dodge, saw it, he was not amused. He came fuming up the mountain and gave Bruce a can of black paint and ordered the sign's immediate removal. Bruce did a fast job of painting out Gus' monument. We didn't laugh when the warden made us pay for the black paint."

The friends that John made on that mountain top sympathized with his desire to become an Olympic skier. They recognized he was not skiing only for the fun of it as they were; they were reminded of his ambition every time he left them behind on the slopes. When they witnessed his Allais-style schussing, high-speed descents they had never seen before, they realized that they were skiing with an Olympic-class skier in training.

Leaving Mount Washington for a month-long stay before continuing to New York where he would once again depart for South America. He intended to keep up his training, do some more racing and keep his promise to return to the ski country where he had first won international acclaim. "The Chileans had invited both Emile and me back, with an offer to ski in any of their competitions and tour the country as far south as Tierra Del Feugo." The timing was right; John was ready to accept the invitation. "All I had to do was get there. The Chilean Ski Federation would take care of me after that."

Allais too was going to Portillo. He was journeying first class; not so John. It was like old times; as usual, he was just about broke. He had only enough for the fare to New York City; a borrowed $200 and a bus ticket.

It was back to the hotel on 42nd street for John, but this time not to Coney Island; he was dishing out Howard Johnson's 28 flavours of ice cream in Queens. After two weeks' fruitless search for a ship to take him to South America, he came up with an agreement with Skyways International, an unscheduled airline that flew DC3's from Miami to South America. In return for publicity for the airline, they would fly John to Chile and back.

He spent his days searching for a newspaper that would carry his story and give it enough coverage to satisfy Skyways; a tall order indeed. A cold call to the sports desk of the New York Times got him meeting with Frank Elkins, the paper's sports editor; his story was published to Skyways' satisfaction.

Elkins, as a followup, arranged for a photo session in Miami when John, boarded the aircraft with boots over his shoulder and skis in hand. Also through the kindness of Mr. Elkins, he met the famous news broadcaster and commentator Lowell Thomas, who had visited Mont Tremblent in previous years and was delighted to have John on his show.They talked about John's exploits in Chile and about skiing and tourism in Canada as well. John once again was an unofficial goodwill ski-ambassador for Canada.

It was a 48 hour bus ride to Miami. The trip was long but not with out a little comic relief. John recalls how, when asked about the skis he was carrying, he shocked people with his deadpan response: "Doesn't every one go skiing in Florida in June?"

The journey from Miami was much faster than the passage by sea. "We visited more ports," John recalls. "In the three days the flight took we stopped at Kingston, Jamaica; Panama; Bogota, Colombia; Lima, Peru; Arica, Chile and finally Santiago." John was thankful that he had made a "white collar deal" with the airline, imagining otherwise he might have been out polishing the aluminum skin of the aircraft at every stop. He was back in Santiago, arriving, as far as he was concerned, first class. Even Allais could not say that he arrived on a private flight.

He made his way on the little train to Portillo, where he joined Emile and his wife, Georgette. The Refugio that had formerly housed the skiers was now, ominously, an army barracks. The hotel that was under construction when John was last there would be their "Refugio" in Portillo.

John skiied with Emile, displaying the same fervour as he had in training sessions in Canada. Emile was pleased to see more improvement in John's skiing; he won six of the eight races, all by a wide margin. Emile was sure that John would be elevated from alternate to full-fledged starter on his Canadian ski team.

John felt even more secure about his making the team when Joe Ryan, the developer of Mount Tremblant, telephoned him from Canada. Ryan asked that John take charge of developing the north side of the mountain when he returned from Chile. John responded that it might be impossible, as he was totally committed to making the Canadian team. A second call from Mr. Ryan changed his mind in a hurry; he sweetened his offer by telling John that he would become his patron. He would pay the $1000 that the Canadian Amateur Ski Association required when one is named to the Olympic team. He also said that he was going to donate another $4000 to the Association. John was floating on a cloud. He believed that now, with Emile Allais' support and Ryan's patronage, a place on the Olympic team was but a month and a DC3 flight away.

The Chilean Ski Federation, superb hosts that they were, invited John, Emile and Georgette to a month of skiing and touring through the lake and volcano country north of Tierra del Fuego. In return, they were to give demonstrations and lessons at the various ski clubs, lodges and hotels along the way.

Many of the resorts were located at the base of glacier-capped volcanoes. "We had a chance to climb some of them. There were guides available to show us the way up but when we showed them how we intended to come down they let us have the mountain to ourselves."

The group, now enlarged by one, a young lady whom Georgette had invited along to ski with John and to round out the foursome, climbed four mountains in all. "The base of most of the mountains was at the 3000 feet and a climb of 9000 more feet to the summit brought us to an altitude near 12,000 feet. Like the carrot in front of the lagging mule, the only thing that kept us moving uphill was the anticipation of the downhill run from the top of the world."

"I can't remember exactly which mountain it was, but we had to leave our warm beds around midnight to start the climb. We were each loaded down with a backpack of food, ropes and climbing paraphernalia. We wore sealskins on our skis for the climb. On this particular climb it was 40 degrees F below zero and getting colder as we neared the top. We were just about frozen when, around noon, we reached the summit. Fortunately for us, the volcano was active, and we were able to climb over the edge inside the cone where we quickly warmed up, staring down at the red lava bubbling and boiling hundreds of feet below."

"We found ourselves skiing between crevasses and over pitches of solid ice that led into sun-swept fields of loose bright powder. On a single run we encountered every possible condition and form that snow could take. I never tired of watching Emile the master schuss those magnificent Andes."

An equally memorable part of the trip was the opportunity to partake in another passion of his life . . . fishing. A guide rowed them around a clear cold mountain lake while they pulled in one lake trout after another, all five to eight pounds. This was done with a short length of string, a broken teaspoon as a lure, and a bent pin for a hook. "We ate lake trout most every night for dinner. Southern Chile could be the resort center of the world if it wasn't so hard to get to."

CHAPTER 9
Olympic Training

Emile and his lovely wife Georgette left South America before the winter was over. They had to make a trip back to France before coming to Canada for the ski season. It was now time for John to take his leave of South America. Making his way to the Skyways International office, John was as happy as he had ever been; he had very little money, but he had a flight back to Miami, and the prospect of being on the Canadian Olympic team was all sewn up.

Skyways' guarantee of a flight home looked as if it was about to go the way of many a promise. The Airline had been caught running guns into Paraguay and had lost its licence to carry passengers. John pleaded with them to get him home. The thought of having to thumb his way home was to much to bear. The Airline was sorry, they could not even carry a non-paying passenger. With the ingenuity that had successfully got him out of other tight situations, John suggested, "How about hiring me as a flight attendant or a freight handler or something like that?" This was more like it. They were scheduled to fly three race horses to Miami in a few days; he could have the job of "horse holder" on take-offs and landings. So John was hired on as official horse holder for Skyways Airline for the flight home the following week.

When John reported for flight duty he was more than a little relieved to hear that the horses would not be taking the trip, but he, as an employee, could leave without them. The flight to Miami, with fewer stops along the way, was much faster. He tried to sign on with another north-bound airline but could not find any takers. The twenty-two dollars in his pocket was just enough for Greyhound fare up the coast to New York, leaving him one dollar for coffee and doughnuts on the 48 hour trip. Arriving in New York, he spent his last 10 cents to call a friend who lent him the bus fare to Ottawa. He arrived the next evening in Ottawa, tired, penniless, but satisfied; home now and the Olympic team next on his agenda.

In the autumn of 1947, the invitation finally came. He was asked to report to the Val Cartier Lodge, near Quebec City by the 15th of December. He was to join the Olympic team for training with coach Emile Allais. Even better, his brother Harvey was also invited to the team's training session. It was going to be the Clifford brothers against the world.

Allais happily greeted John when he arrived at the team's hotel in Val Cartier. In his best English, Emile reminded John that he had assured him a place on the team months before. After days of high speed training on the Val Cartier slopes, the first of the disappointments to beset John was handed to him; when the team members were named, John was designated an alternate; he was not to be a starter. His training runs had been good, his time had been just split seconds from the top. But it was those split seconds that separated him from the chosen starters. He would go to St. Moritz, but would not compete unless he had to replace an injured team member. It was at the end of the training session that John received the second disappointment, the disappointment that to this day he feels was the toughest of his life to swallow.

Fall 1947, leaving for Olympic training: Art Tommy, Fred Clifford, John Clifford

Sydney Dawes, President of the Canadian Amateur Ski Association, and Canada's Olympic Committee representative, had the final say on the makeup of the Olympic team. He was the same man who had wished John Godspeed on his first trip to Chile. He called John from Montreal and told him that he was not to go. John was incredulous. After being given the team's clothing and a passport, after swallowing his pride and accepting the position of alternate, he was being refused a place on the team. He had difficulty holding the phone to his ear, as he listened; he could not believe his ears. When he asked why, Dawes replied: "You're too old John!" At 25 years he was too old? The coach himself found it hard to believe when John gave him the news. Both men agreed that there had to be another reason for the dismissal.

"Old age" was too implausible. As hard as he tried, Allais was unable to convince Dawes of his error.

John now had two goals: to find out why Dawes had denied him his rightful place on the team...and to prove that he was capable of being a champion, one of the best in Canada, if not the world, even though he was an ancient of 25 years.

John returned to Ottawa emotionally torn and depressed. He did not feel up to his work at Camp Fortune. Needing a new challenge, something to change his negative mind-set, he contacted Joe Ryan at Mount Tremblant, accepting his offer to take charge of the north side's development. Ryan was happy to hear that John would be on the job sooner than expected, and urgeed him to come as soon as possible. There

was something peculiar in Ryan's tone; John realized, after hanging up, that he had sounded unsurprised that John was available earlier than expected.

There was much to do in preparation for his departure for Mont Tremblant. First, and of great importance, was to make sure that his concession to build, operate and maintain the tows at Camp Fortune continued uninterrupted. To facilitate this, he formed the first of the many partnerships of his business career. With Steve Saunders, his assistant and a very capable mechanic, he formed the company Clifford & Saunders, whose sole mandate would be the operating of Camp Fortune that winter.

John and Harvey at Val Cartier, 1947.

CHAPTER 10
Mont Tremblant

Arriving at Ryan's Mont Tremblant resort in late December, 1947, John found that some of the work on the mountain's north side was already underway, but there was still much to do. There were trails to cut, two rope tows to improve and the completion of the top and bottom terminals of the Roebling single chairlift. Ryan wanted the job finished for spring skiing that same season. This was the kind of challenge John needed.

With a hard-working crew of 25 men, John started cutting the trails whose names have become familiar to skiers around the world. The Lowell Thomas, the Devil's River and the Sissy Schuss were all cut under the direction of the Night Rider from Camp Fortune. At the same time, under John's direction, the chairlift was completed. The target date for the opening of the north side was the weekend of March 3rd, 1948. On the 1st of March, all that remained to be done was the installation of a telephone system linking the top and bottom terminals of the Roebling chairlift. On the morning of the 2nd of March this was completed. John spent the remaining daylight hours testing and re-testing the lift and the new downhill runs.

His work crew saw for the first time that he was not just an inspired technician, but an extremely talented skier as well. John lays claim to the honour of not only creating those famous north-side trails, but being the first to ski them as well. He noticed that during these test runs Mr.Joe Ryan was watching him, like a race horse owner watching his thoroughbred working out on the track.

John was thankful that there was still some good skiing to be had for the remainder of the spring season after the grand opening. He had not forgotten his mission of proving that he had been wrongly rejected by the Olympic team, which had yet to prove itself. He skied Tremblant for the remainder of the season like a man possessed. He skied with the dedication and discipline of a training racer, not as a disappointed alternate let go by the team. He skied, clinging to the hope that he might, by some miracle, still be called to ski for Canada.

"I was living at the newly-completed Devil's River Lodge with Mr. and Mrs. Charlie Duncan and their six-year-old son, Peter. Their warm company and support was very encouraging during the days of hard work that I was doing for the first time as a professional, outside of Camp Fortune. I may have been considered too old for the Olympics, but in truth I was very young, experience-wise, in the world of business, particularly as Joe Ryan saw it."

The call never came. The 1948 Winter Olympics went into the record book, but John could not let go. Was he really dropped from the team because of his age, or was it for other reasons as he suspected? An incident that occured while working for Joe Ryan presented him with the probable answer.

One evening, after a hard day's work, he was enjoying the cosy warmth of the Duncan's fireplace when a telephone call came from Mrs. Ryan. She told John that she had not seen her husband for more than a week, which was not all that unusual - almost everyone knew that he disappeared from time-to-time for a few days of drinking. This time, Mrs. Ryan urgently insisted was different. "I know his pattern," she said. "He may be gone a few days but never as long as this." Knowing that he sometimes became lost when he had had too much, she was concerned for his safety.

With Ernie McCulloch, the head of the Tremblant ski school, John set out to find their boss. It did not take much detective work to find him; Ryan had left an obvious trail of high spending and copious drinking behind him. The local bars chose to put such a prominent man up for the night rather than risk his ire by tossing him out or taking him home. "When Ernie and I found him, he was in pretty bad shape. We decided that it would be better to sober him up before delivering him to Mrs. Ryan, so we took him back for a cold bath and hot coffee at Devil's River Lodge."

It was during the sobering-up process that John got a clue to the real reason for his being dropped from the team. Complaining of being forced into a cold bath, Joe Ryan said in a loud threatening voice,"Leave me alone or I'll throw you out same as I threw out your other boss." John could not understand what Ryan meant by his "other boss", but Ernie suggested he might be referring to the Olympic Team's boss, Sydney Dawes. While the team was in training at Val Cartier, Dawes was guest at

Ryan"s Mount Tremblant Lodge. During another bout of drinking, Ryan demanded, for no apparent reason, that Dawes leave the premises; according to Ernie, to depart immediately, bag and baggage, out into the cold night and never to come back.

With this small piece of information, John was able to get Ryan to unfold the rest of the story. After his eviction, Ryan told him, the furious Mr. Dawes returned his Olympic donation of $5000, without explanation. This meant that John had lost his sponsor. Ryan was certain that this was the real reason that he had been dropped from the team.

John felt that there was no point in trying to prove that this was the true reason for his being bumped from the team. In his own mind there was no doubt about it. He was relieved; his doubts on that score settled, all that remained was to prove that had he been on the team, he would have been a winner.

Spring, always a short season in the Laurentians, turned quickly into hot summer. The Devil's River at the base of Tremblant swelled with the melted runoff. The competitive season in Canada was over; John would have to wait until the next winter to test himself.

To keep himself in condition over the summer months, he took on a job with the Harold Taggart Construction Company as night foreman looking after the excavation for the new government DVA building on Ottawa's Sparks Street. The excavation was in solid limestone and John learned about short period blasting techniques. His teachers from CIL were impressed by his quick ability to absorb what they taught him. The lessons he learned were to be useful in John's future, and in the future of ski area development in Canada.

John became concerned that his position of supervising up to a hundred men driving bulldozers and trucks was not letting him condition himself as he intended. Too much desk work and not enough physical labor was not to his liking, so, whenever there was a lull in the paper work, he got out there and swung pick and shovel along with his men.

The following winter of 1949 John returned to Camp Fortune where he continued to operate and improve the area's facilities. His disappointment at being dropped from the '48 team still rankled. He still wanted more than anything to race against the best in the world, to prove that he was good enough to be champion. Would he be able to repeat his South American accomplishment here on home soil? The answer could only be found in head-to-head on-hill competition. Did he just want to get even, or was this a healthy desire to compete and win?

John with Rheal Seguin,
Claude Ritcher,
Bob Gratton.

He was in top physical condition when he returned to Camp Fortune after his summer digging in the Sparks street hole, and the quality of his skiing was never better. The season's slate of competitions was falling into place as if he had arranged it himself. The French team, which had run away with the '48 Olympics, was going to race at Mont Tremblant, at his hill, later in the winter. The races were to be known as the "Closed Canadian Championships." He was not going to miss that event.

With the goal of winning the Canadian Closed, John raced in every event that he could. The Night Riders watched John ski without knowing the real reason behind his extraordinary drive. He won or placed in every club and zone race he entered. He won the Alpine combined at the Central Canadian Championships at Camp Fortune. When the Canadian Closed Championships came, he was ready.

Race day at Mont Tremblant was a glorious sight: flags and banners were flying, the French team was there, basking in Olympic glory. Olympic downhill champion Henri Orrelier was present, and making sure that everyone was aware of the fact. He was the man John targeted to beat to rid himself of the pain he carried within him. He believes to this day that he was never so fired up, so intense, prior to a race.

He skiied the race as he had never before skiied. He visualized himself, during the flashing descent, speeding down the Roca Jack high in the Andes, and as the Roca Jack flashed through his mind, images of Tuckermans and the Headwall also swept by. "That bump, Fripps Folly, like the one at the ravine . . . the next turn . . . easy . . .

same as dodging a crevasse . . . crouch lower . . . follow Emile." John crossed the finish line in such a state that he was literally unsure which country he was in.

He had beaten most of the French team, including the Olympic Champion Henri Orrelier. He told the uncomprehending media, "If I die tomorrow, I can die satisfied." He had beaten the best. With the downhill behind him, the slalom, held the following day, was easy. He did not have to win it to come up with the combined title. The nagging question, as far as he was concerned, had been answered. One year after the St. Moritz '48 Olympics, John Clifford had won his own Olympic race.

The 1949 ski season closed on this happy note. Having laid his ghosts to rest, he now had to seriously think about his future. He fully intended to keep on skiing but, as enjoyable as it was, it could not earn him a living. His concession to run the tows at Camp Fortune just covered his winter living expenses, so what about the rest of the year?

Bob Gratton, John, Clifford, Bob Irving, Claude Ritcher.

CHAPTER 11
1951: Winless in Colorado

Margaret Phillips, a former schoolmate at Glebe Collegiate, came into John's life. She was the daughter of Pat and Eddy Phillips, a member of a family of some athletic prominence. Her father Ed was a member of the Ottawa Rough Riders' football team. Marg was a winning competitor as well. The Glebe's ski team was fortunate to count her as a member during most of the years she attended the school.

After a stint with the women's division of the RCAF in Dartmouth Nova Scotia, Margaret graduated from the University of Toronto as a Physical Education specialist. At the time of John's advances, she was teaching at the Glebe in Ottawa, and was also an active member of the Ottawa Ski Club where they became more than just friends.

Their courtship in marriage in July of 1951 at Ottawa's Trinity Anglican Church. The reception was given by their friends John and Ginny Fripp. John Fripp was the Director of the Mont Tremblant ski school and one of Canada's great skiers. During the reception, Fripp took John aside to ask him to come to Mont Tremblant to teach skiing. John's loyalty to Camp Fortune, and an invitation from Mr. Lyle Beamish to develop a ski hill for him near Ottawa, forced him to refuse.

Their honeymoon was very short as John had a summer business needing his attention. With permission from the city of Ottawa, he had opened a waterski club and school at Britannia Pier in the west end. He had given many lessons that spring when in July, with the business well underway, the water got very rough, too rough for students. Daily strong winds finally forced him to move the school from the pier to the more sheltered area of Clearview, just below Black Rapids on the Rideau.

One of the students who was sorry to see John take his school away was Jeff

Crain, a great snow-skier and quarterback of the Winnipeg Blue Bombers. "Jeff came to see us on one of those very windy days," John recalls. "The waves on Lake Deschene were being beaten into frothing whitecaps, but Jeff insisted we go out." Finding some smoother water out behind a log boom some distance away, they began the lesson. "I was amazed when Jeff, who had never waterskiied before, learned to ski on two skis, on one ski, and then, backwards on one ski, including a backward deep start on one ski. All of this in only one and a half hours!"

The waterski school, with John as chief instructor, was so successful in its new location that, in the second summer, the Cliffords purchased a cottage nearby on the Rideau River. He and his bride moved into the little cottage on the river and looked forward to living there happily.

With a successful summer behind them and the cooler weather fast approaching, they closed the school for the season. As soon as the water-skis were put away, John was off to close the promised Beamish hill deal.

Lyle Beamish had contacted John just before his wedding. He wanted to create a ski area on a piece of property that he owned at the base of King Mountain on the west side of the Gatineau Park escarpment. The hill, with its 400 vertical feet, was only 12 miles from downtown Ottawa. John was concerned about the its southwest exposure and reluctantly agreed to Beamish's choice of location, preffering another area that was closer to Camp Fortune, with a better easterly exposure.

Mr. Beamish had a very strong argument for his selection. He not only owned the hill, he had a cottage on nearby King Mountain and he had acquired some 500 acres around an artificial lake for a future subdivision. Despite the disadvantage of mediocre snow, easy access with adequate parking and electricity readily available for night skiing made Beamish Hill the optimum choice. With Mr. Beamish's funding a chalet was built, the hill prepared and the Clifford and Saunders Company installed three rope tows, all in time for the 1951-52 winter season. John would often says, "Clifford and Saunders left Mr. Beamish...beaming!"

With John's Mont Tremblant win still fresh in the 1949 CASA record book, he was invited to race on the 1950 FIS team, the team that would be competing for the world championships in Aspen, Colorado.

The snow had not yet fallen in the east when the chosen skiers left for Aspen. "There we were, ready to go . . . no snow, no training...no money, no transportation." There was no way to solve the first problems but John pressed his 1947 Mercury into service and drove fellow team members Alex MacDougal, Andy Tommy and Jim

Georges all the way to Aspen. They made it, but it was close – it had been a long tedious trip that tested their dedication to skiing, and tempers were very short.

"We didn't do well in the world championships; after all, we arrived one day and had to ski the next, and we had not been on our skis yet that season." There were many trial runs where the Canadians' best was not good enough, but John placed a poor second against a Norwegian team skier in one of the warm-up races, held at the Winterpark ski area.

Then it was back into the crowded Merc for the long trip home. On the way they intended to take a shot at the North American Championships in Banff, Alberta.

1950: the Canadian team at the World Championships in Aspen, Colorado.

Unhappy as they were with the long drive, they were also angry with their host, George Encil, the owner of the Banff area where the races were held. He had chartered an aircraft fly all the Europeans up to Banff for the competition. He did not offer his countrymen even the opportunity to refuse a flight to Calgary. Granted, it was Encil's first chance to test his facilities for an international race, but he was lucky to have any Canadians competing at all. John and his fellow Canadians, though they didn't show it, felt slighted by the treatment the others were getting.

The team arrived in Banff in a state of total exhaustion. They had a few days of training prior to the race under "coach" Harvey Clifford, John's brother. He was the manager and ski school director. It was like old times for John, skiing and racing with his brother and still not able to beat him! The Canadians did not do well; they came away from the race depressed and shaken by the beating that they had taken. It was going to be a long drive home and it looked as if international racing had seen the last of John Clifford.

The return trip from Banff was marred by a major blizzard that marooned them for three days in a small North Dakota town. The little hotel where they waited out the storm had only a pool table to keep them occupied. With no funds available for betting, skis, boots and goggles frequently changed hands.

CHAPTER 12
Greener Pastures

The ski tow and its various derivatives has been given the credit for developing the ski business into the huge industry it is today. In its infancy, ski tow technology in the early 50's was crude if not dangerous. Much still had to be worked out in matters of construction and safety. Many skier accidents occurred; clothing and scarves, sometimes even long flowing hair could be entangled in the rope as it pulled the unwary skier up the slope. The possibility of accidental injury, and the strength required to ride the tow, hindered its complete public acceptance.

There were many members of the ski world who still distanced themselves from the tows, staying with cross-country trail skiing. Many skiers of the old school preferred to climb, as John and his pocketbook were finding out. The expenses of operating a tow still outweighed revenues. As much as he loved his winter work, he was awakening to the possibility that greener pastures might exist beyond the confines of Camp Fortune.

Summer months were now more than just in-between seasons for John. He was not earning enough with his tow business to relax and await the next winter's return. Luckily, there was always a friend or acquaintance made during the winter, who, recognising his talents, had some kind of summer job waiting for him.

Digby Viets was one such person. He was responsible for introducing John to the business side of golf. John had been a caddy in his boyhood, and still played the occasional game, but this was business. Viets asked for John's help in building Ottawa's first miniature golf and driving range on the Prescott highway at Hogsback. With the stipulation that he and Margaret would keep the waterski school in operation, John helped build and operate the golfing project. His business association with Mr. Viets continued successfully for the next five years.

Thousands of people from the Ottawa area enjoyed the range. The then new concept of supplying free golf balls and a driver was as revolutionary as riding up a hill on a tow in winter. Invitations were sent out to all the golf clubs in the surrounding area, suggesting that the pros bring their clients to the range to give them lessons. Many did, and in return, Digby and John were invited to play at their courses. "I did not play as well as I'd have liked to." One of the pros suggested he wear glasses, and his game vastly improved. He had been too proud to wear glasses while racing on skis, and when he saw how much his game improved when he took the advice, he wondered: "Could this be the reason for those split-second, second place finishes?" He decided that he would swallow his pride and wear glasses in his next race.

John's quiet unassuming manner easily made him friends. Many say that it was his temperament that attracted them. John thinks that may have been so, but he thinks it was really his penchant for telling stories of his winter adventures. It did not matter that they were playing golf under the hot sun, John was always ready to tell the uninitiated of his adventures in skiing and the joy of participating in the sport. His belief in skiing's future was obvious.

John's expertise in ski development was not limited to the cutting of trails and the installation of tows. Four-way skiing was the direction that skiing and ski competition took after the end of the war. A really aggressive, competitive skier had to be competent in downhill and slalom and in cross-country and jumping as well. A firm believer in four-way skiing, in the development of "real" skiers, John obtained permission to build a 25-meter jump with a small tower in Paradise Valley behind Fortune Lodge. This jump, designed for the beginner, was completed with the help of the Night Riders, most of whom enjoyed the thrill of jumping, of flying without wings. John was correct in his theory that any skier who could jump could be a competitor in all four ski disciplines. Many Ottawa Ski Club members, starting on John's smaller jump, graduated to larger facilities, and active jumpers of that era often went on to become top all-round competitors.

The work that John did on the larger Lockeberg 60-meter jump was also a first for Camp Fortune. This jump, originally built by one of the founders of the OSC, needed repair and modification. Longer jumps resulting from better training required a longer landing area. A new, artificial landing had to be constructed. Blasting and bulldozing of the hill to accommodate the landing platform, along with the cedar supporting poles and planking, were the only expenses to the Ottawa Ski Club. John cajoled volunteer help from the club's members by offering a free season pass in return for ten weekends of work. A tall order for volunteers, it was more like a sentence: twenty days at hard labour. The club absorbed half of the cost of the pass, Clifford and Saunders the balance.

A jump like the Lockeberg was not complete without a judge's stand, and this one had to be 45 feet high. The supporting poles had to be spliced together to make them

long enough. Not surpisingly, there was a shortage of climbers around when the need arose. Fortunately, an experienced telephone linesman named Alex MacDougall volunteered, and he and John completed the high climbing and rigging, drilling and bolting the framework together.

Alex MacDougal had quite a laugh when John told him of his climbing experience when he was a few years younger. "There was a wealthy man by the name of Harry McLean who had a great sense of humour. He liked to give money away, but if you wanted to be on the receiving end, you had to earn it. He was in one of his give-away moods when he advertised a $100 prize for anyone who could scale a 35-foot greasy pole. The contest was up Merrickville way. I had a car and just about enough gas in it to get there. I gathered up two friends, John Bergeron and Knobby Walsh, to go along. They were short of gas money as well, but they were sure that they would be able to climb the pole and win the money for the trip home. They hardly got off the ground. I must have been highly motivated by the thought of the empty gas tank and the long walk home; I made it to within 5 feet of the top ...and won. The $100 was mine."

The modified Lockeberg jump became a fixture at Camp Fortune for many years. Many a competition was won or lost on its in-run and graceful landing surface. Over time, the younger members of the club accepted the "old" jump's presence as if it had always been there.

As time passed, John was asked to use his jump construction experience as a consultant in the erection of many such facilities across Canada, the foremost being Big Thunder at the Little Norway ski area at the Lakehead.

With the world-class Lockeberg jump now part of Fortune's facilities, the club needed more than its 300-ft. Cote du Nord hill for downhill training. John suggested that he could lay out a suitable trail with an 800-foot vertical drop on King Mountain. Such a run would offer the club's skiers downhill experience that would put them at the top of the winner's list in any Zone race.

He sold his plan for the new downhill trail to the club's directors, and it was subsequently cut. The King Mountain run, along with the jumps, the serviced slopes and the many cross-country trails joining the various lodges, made Camp Fortune complete. It was becoming the perfect incubator for the racers, the winners, the world beaters that it is famous for.

With all the construction that John was involved with that winter, he still made time for a little competitive skiing. This was also the winter that he was wearing the special glasses which he had used when playing golf the past summer. To test his theory that the glasses may have been the difference between winning and losing, he entered the Province of Quebec Slalom Championships at Val Cartier. Wearing the glasses, he won, but not without incident: during a practice run he pulled an ankle, but the perfect snow conditions on the day of the race allowed him to compete with only a little pain. The win gave him the opportunity to attend the Olympic try-outs in Banff right after the Val Cartier race.

The snow conditions in the Rockies, on the very steep Mount Norquay, where the trials were held, were hard, fast and icy; very different than back east a few days earlier. His injured ankle could not take the pounding over the hard icy course. He ended a poor sixth: not good enough to make the team, though, as once before he was named a spare. The pain was intense; a medical examination revealed that he had raced on a cracked bone. Favouring the ankle had cost him the race, or at least a better placing.

CHAPTER 13
Politics and Performing

At the start of the waterski school's third year, John's peaceful bubble burst. Politics, a nemesis that was to follow him most of his business career, raised its ugly head for the first time. "When I went to renew my permit I was told that I would have to have a petition of approval signed by the thirty residents who lived nearby. This after two years of super neighbourly relations; I had actually given some of them free lessons!"

The question was asked, and there was only one dissenter. Twenty-nine were in favour, yet John needed unanimous consent if he was to continue. As hard as he pleaded his case to the authorities, permission was refused. "Politically," John said, "That dissenter must have been mighty powerful." The waterski school was forced to relocate.

They moved the school to the waters of the Ottawa Rowing Club on the Ottawa River. Here, because of his past association with the club, they were received with open arms. Anxious to get the season under way, John constructed a $2000 adjustable waterski jump before realizing the site was unsafe; the river current carried logs and sewage through the ski zone.

The school had to move once again; first to Mooney's Bay, and eventually to Rideau Glen Lodge above Black Rapids. During the next five years, John taught more than 300 people the skills of waterskiing. As waterski schools go, the Cliffords were running one of the best in the east, but teaching was not enough to satisfy John's lust for excitement.

Publicity was the most effective method of obtaining waterski students and, running against the grain of his inherent modesty, John became a showman. He

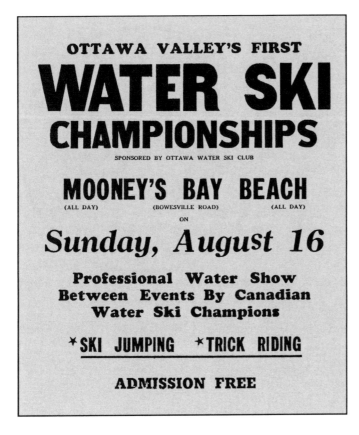

OTTAWA VALLEY'S FIRST

WATER SKI
CHAMPIONSHIPS

SPONSORED BY OTTAWA WATER SKI CLUB

MOONEY'S BAY BEACH
(ALL DAY)   (BOWESVILLE ROAD)   (ALL DAY)

ON

Sunday, August 16

Professional Water Show Between Events By Canadian Water Ski Champions

★ SKI JUMPING   ★ TRICK RIDING

ADMISSION FREE

found it difficult to "mind the store" while at the same time putting on demonstrations at every regatta in Eastern Ontario.

Steve Saunders built a powerful inboard boat, and designed and installed innovative towing equipment that became industry standards. Clifford and Saunders were as inventive on the water as they were on the snow. The school put together a group of skiers who presented a spectacular show. With high speed turns, spins and jumps, the audience loved them wherever they went.

John did not overlook waterskiing competition. Finding time for competition during the summer was as difficult as in winter, but he made the time. It was business as usual, and competition as well.

Before retiring from waterskiing in 1956, John won the Quebec waterski championships four times. In 1954 he represented Canada at the world championships held at the CNE in Toronto, where he placed sixth in the combined. The next year he won the overall Canadian championship. He was one of the first to do one-ski turn-arounds on water and helicopter spins off the jump in competition.

1956 was a singular year for John. He decided to try to become the only man in Canada to win both a waterski championship and a downhill championship within a year. Having won the Canadian combined waterski title at the CNE earlier in the fall, he entered the Canadian Championships that winter at Blue Mountain, Collingwood, Ontario, winning his specialty, the combined.

The Dieppe Trail, used for the Downhill at Blue Mountain, was a narrow, treacherous run. A miss on any turn could put a racer into the woods with an injury. Ottawa skiers proved themselves capable, making the meet a clean sweep. John, looking for a combined win, had to calculate just how good a time would be necessary in each event. First place was not necessary, as a fast second place in both events could give him a win.

Glen Fraser of the OSC had the fastest time in the downhill, beating John by seven tenths of a second. Shawn Fripp, another lad from Ottawa, won the slalom, beating John by a split second after two runs. John's combined time gave him the Canadian combined title. He had mixed water and snow and come out with a winning combination. Linda Crutchfield, in the 70's, has been the only other person to duplicate this feat to date.

John closed out his professional waterskiing career with an attempt to break the world's one-ski distance record of 100 miles. With Dave Hyman, a good friend and an enthusiastic waterskier, they set off from Hogsback to Black Rapids and back. "We had estimated that we would have to cover that stretch of river ten times," John recalls. "Well, we didn't get very far. After two round trips, Dave fell off and when Steve turned around to pick him up he hit a log, severely damaging the prop and drive shaft which put an end to the endurance attempt." It also was the end of an era for John; waterskiing became an avocation rather than a vocation from that point on.

John and Marg had to give up the little cottage on the river when the waterski school moved back to the river near the Ottawa Rowing Club. Needless to say, getting the school underway in the new location, building the water ski jump and attending his night work was very demanding, but somehow John was able to stretch a 24-hour day to the maximum. To prove it, with all the projects he had going at the time, he was still able to recruit volunteers to help him build a two-room cabin on Kingsmere road near Camp Fortune. Ted Crain, one of the friends who helped, was the first to say that, "If John could not get to a frontier to live in, he would bring the frontier to Ottawa."

The cabin was more like a pioneer's home than a full-time abode just over the river from the Nation's Capital. It had a hand-dug well with a hand pump and a backhouse for plumbing. He is quick to add that they did not have much more on their farm in New Brunswick. John's only concession to the modern era was the electricity for a few lights and appliances.

The little house on Kingsmere road was not what the Cliffords had been used to, but it was the closest to Camp Fortune that he could live at the time. The Clifford's daughter Betsy may not remember living there but it was the home that first welcomed her after her birth at the Ottawa Civic Hospital. It was also not far from the off-season job with the National Capital Commission that John was also holding down.

In 1953, the Ottawa news papers were full of the NCC's plans to construct a limited-access scenic parkway north from Hull through Gatineau Park, passing near Camp Fortune and on to the Champlain Lookout, where it would terminate. With skiing and his tow concession at Camp Fortune not paying very handsomely during

1956, the Canadian Championships at Blue Mountain, Collingwood. Rear: Rick Marshall, (name unknown), John Gill, Glen Fraser, Shawn Fripp. Front: Bob Gratton, Reg LeFebvre, Dick Porter, John Clifford.

the winter months, and the uncertainty of summer employment always a threat, John decided to apply for a general foreman's position with the NCC. He was hired, and for the next five years he was Head Engineer Peter Ackroyd's assistant. "Peter Ackroyd was a hell of an engineer and a very happy man with a great sense of humor." John recalls, "I guess his son Danny, the actor-comedian, inherited his talent from his dad."

Some of the projects that John worked on were the two-mile Lac De Fee Parkway; nine miles of the Gatineau Parkway; Philip Lake access road; Ridge road to the fire tower at the north end of Gatineau Park; the access road to Camp Fortune; surveying and building stone parapets and lookouts at the Gatineau Parkway's northern terminus; Champlain Lookout, as well as opening many gravel pits and rock quarries. John considered the five years spent with the NCC and Peter Ackroyd his university years; an education that he valued the rest of his life.

Competitive skiing during the winter of '53 was at the Zone and club level. No matter how busy he was, the lure of the race was too tempting to pass up. He continued to do well even with little serious training. Winning the Zone's Christophe Klotz memorial trophy, and a good second-place finish in the 4-way Norland Challenge Cup, satisfied his competitive spirit that season.

In 1954, Mr. Fred Bronson, the former Chairman of the Federal District Commission which eventually became the National Capital Commission, suggested that John take a look at the possibility of turning an area on Lake Harrington, known as the Edwards Estate, into a ski resort. This was his opportunity to step out of the confines of Fortune; John could see the Edwards estate as his stepping stone into major ski area development. He envisioned his name alongside Tremblant's Ryan and Banff's Encil.

He enlisted the aid of two of his friends, lawyers Russ Smart and Bert Lawrence. These men, members of the Ottawa Ski Club, gladly accepted the invitation to help John explore the Edwards Estate possibilities. Although he never said as much, John felt that they too would be helping their careers along with the publicity that such a development would create.

The three men walked and explored every inch of the mountainside. When they were satisfied that they had taken into account every possible factor, they laid out a plan on paper, and, because they were so sure of the government's acceptance, they actually went out and cut a pilot line with a vertical drop of 600 feet, for the chairlift. They prepared a very detailed brief and submitted it to the commission.

Their proposal was turned down in favour of turning the Harrington Lake property into a permanent summer residence for Canada's Prime Ministers. The one thing they had overlooked was beyond their control; politics. John was learning that politics and skiing make a poor mixture.

The Gatineau Ski Zone, wanting to create world class jumpers, planned to build a training jump in Ottawa's Rockcliffe Park area. The previous jump had been torn down during the war. Mr. Odd Michaelson, the Zone's jumping chairman, asked John for his advice and his assistance in building a new and larger jumping facility. Once again John solicited the help of his buddy Russ Smart. his time the threesome's motivation was the genuine belief that Ottawa needed a world class jump to bolster the rapidly declining sport of jumping. A first-class jumping hill, allowing spectacular performances, would attract new devotees to the sport.

Many truckloads of fill were brought in and dumped on the landing hill where it was re-contoured to carefully laid-out specifications by volunteers with shovels. Russ Smart, looking from far below at all the workers scattered about during this stage of the landing's construction, was heard to say: "We're not building a jump, we're building a giant ant hill!" The jump's tower was unique. In order to extend the in-run, a portion of of the new tower had to cross a roadway. This was not a major problem, as the road was not used during the winter. The new tower was designed with a small removeable section to allow the passage of summer traffic. It was an ingenious answer to the problem; to make the section's removal simple, they constructed the tower of structural steel, rather than wooden beams.

At the opening day party Mayor Charlotte Whitton was invited to cut the ribbon. Her speech shocked them all when they heard her say: "I compliment you on your design, allowing the tower to be removed when the snow disappears in the spring." Remove the whole tower? The builders, the Zone officials, even the jumpers who were present could not believe their ears. No one present was able to change her mind. The tower, including the small over-the-road section had to be dismantled at the end of each season. Even worse, the Zone was denied the right to charge an admission fee to cover expenses. In one stroke, the whole enterprise was rendered financially unviable.

The structure was dismantled without ever seeing a major competition. The steel was donated, through John's influence, to the Ottawa Ski Club, where it was later put to good use almost as it had been originally intended. The club built a 30-meter intermediate jump, using the same steel to build the judge's tower. John later installed lighting on the jump, adding to its use and popularity.

CHAPTER 14
The Ottawa Ski Boom

When the five-day government work week was established in 1955, weekend sporting activities skyrocketed. The extra day allowed time for travel, shopping and church-going, as well as recreation. Gone was the the tight fit-it-into-one-day rush. The Ottawa Ski Club's membership had reached a plateau of 2500 to 3000, but in 1955 it began to grow rapidly. Camp Fortune kept John busy installing more and more facilities to accommodate the demand. The club also initiatated new programs, the most popular being free midget instruction. This program encouraged more family skiing and along with it more skier and car traffic.

The NCC finally accepted the club's repeated requests for a better access road. Skier traffic doubled. It looked like a rosy future for the ski industry with the five day week; the ski-lift business might at long last become viable. Ever optimistic, John Clifford was seeing his prophecy of skiing's popularity come to fruition, and he was determined to play a major role in the burgeoning industry.

He heard of a piece of property near Meach Lake that Mr. Henry Gill might be persuaded to sell to the right person. "I was successful in persuading him that I was the right person. The rapid growth of the ski industry and the part I had played in it, and my intention to play an even bigger part in the future, must have helped to convince him." He sold John a cottage on the east side of the lake, along with four acres of land. Moving nearer, he could now devote more time to the development of Camp Fortune while he continued with his job with the NCC.

John entered organized skiing in a big way as soon as the Cliffords settled into their cottage on Meach Lake. In the fall of 1955 he became the president of the Gatineau zone. Having proved that 4-way skiing competition at an early age, was the

62

best method of training the racers of the future, he arranged meetings with the athletic directors of all the Ottawa-Hull high schools to re-organize inter-scholastic ski racing. This important level of skiing was faltering at a time when it should have been at its best.

The meetings that ensued were positive; the schools wanted to compete. Inter-scholastic ski meets, prior to John's stepping in, had primarily been organized by three men with very little help from their schools: John Pringle Taylor, Father Zachary of St. Patrick's College and Ralph Thornton, a teacher at Glebe Collegiate. These men volunteered a great deal of time and effort, and feeling that their efforts were unappreciated, had dropped skiing as an extra-curricular activity.

Another factor handicapping high school skiing was the lack of supervision. The students were sometimes away overnight while attending competitions, often without chaperones. Parents complained, and the schools dropped skiing from their sporting agenda. John was aware that Canada's future competitive position at the world level rested on the youngsters; in effect that schools were the farm teams from which the champions of the future would come.

John was so determined to get a Gatineau area junior program going that he went out on a limb and promised that the Zone would provide all the personnel to run two major competitions a year, including chaperones, if the schools would organize and field the teams.

Two races were introduced - the Dalton Wood and Art Lovett 4-way competitions. True to his word, John provided the Zone's help in running the two events that became the most prestigious school level races held. As he had predicted, many top-flight racers, male and female, came from the program that he chaired for nine years. Many of his 4-way competitors went on to provincial and even national fame.

The high school competition program was aimed at the young up-and-coming skier who had, by one means or another, acquired more than just the basics of skiing. Some may have taught themselves or may have had the little ski school training that was available at the time. John was not satisfied with this limited group of potential skiers. Ski lessons somehow had to be made available to the mass younger generation, not just the lucky few. In 1950 he approached Ottawa's Westboro Kiwanis club, suggesting they make ski lessons available at Beamish hill free of charge or at least at minimal expense.

Under his watchful eye, the Ottawa-Kiwanis ski school was born. The five Ottawa Kiwanis clubs formed the Ottawa Municipal Ski Council under the guidance of John Veit, Gatineau Ski Zone, Alf Dulude, City of Ottawa Parks and Recreation and the Ottawa Citizen, who had John Fripp train three hundred amateur high school and university students to be ski instructors. The instructors received an honorarium of ten dollars per Saturday morning.

The school operated for ten or twelve years, teaching more than three thousand children annually, free of charge. The program was financed by Kiwanis, with many dedicated people helping, including Harold Fawcett. The program graduated thousands of safe recreational skiers and also produced its share of major competitors, all a credit to the sport and a credit to John's foresight and initiative.

In 1951 and 1952 John attended the CASA annual meetings in an effort to persuade the association to allow amateur skiers to earn up to ten dollars per day without losing their amateur status. Until then, a strict interpretation of the rules meant that all the Kiwanis school instructors were ineligible for ammateur competition, including, especially, Olympic competition.

In the winter of 1955 John was keeping a proud eye on a young lady named Anne Heggtveit. Anne had been brought up through the Ottawa Ski Club's junior racing program and the Gatineau Zone racing system. She was on her way to world fame. The highlight of the year was her extraordinary performance at the Holmenkolen Giant Slalom, the Norwegian championship. She was the first and youngest Canadian to win the event. She reinforced John's faith in the OSC junior program; there had to be more like her waiting in the wings.

The factory where Steve Saunders and John produced Canada's first all steel T-Bar lift was Alex MacDonald's Albert Street garage. The Ottawa Ski Club's decision to have John construct a lift on their Herbert Marshall Hill gave the Clifford and Saunders Company the opportunity to build the lift of their dreams...an all-steel construction that would do the company proud.

The timing could not have been better for Clifford and Saunders. The Val Cartier area in Quebec had closed its operation the previous season, and had sold its Constam T-Bar to the Chantecler Lodge in Ste-Adele. John made a quick trip to the Chantecler where he happily found all the T-Bar parts, the bull wheels, the sheaves, frame boxes, cables, everything but the wooden towers that he did not want anyway. He purchased the lot for $6000 and had it shipped to Camp Fortune by truck.

Steve and John started the tower construction at Alex's garage, working every night. The hot July nights were made even hotter by the cutting and welding of the steel for the towers that were to replace the obsolete wooden poles. But it looked as if their meagre resources were also melting; by the end of August, only a month into the project, they were running out of money. Their accountant, Ernie Clarke, unhappily confirmed that they were broke. The towers were ready for erection; the parts from Chantecler were on site . . . and paid for. "We couldn't quit. With only the installation on the hill remaining we had to come up with the cash to finish the job."

John and his good friend Russ Smart came up with the idea of offering business people, doctors, lawyers, dentists, a family seasons pass for 5 years in return for a $500 loan. John was on the telephone the next day quickly proving the plan's worth. He raised over $25,000 in short order. With financing in place and an abundance of volunteer labour, some of whom took advantage of the free pass offer, the lift was completed in time for the 1956 season. The construction crew, consisting of Reg Toomey, Bob Gratton, Ralph Mallory, Tony Smialowski, Alex MacDougal, Ken Nolan, Gordy Dean, Peter Snead and many others, had good reason to celebrate the lift's opening. Clifford and Saunders' hybrid steel-towered Constam T-Bar lift became the prototype for many others throughout Canada as the sport's popularity grew and technology progressed.

John, using this same system of raising money, was able to improve all of the lift systems that he was responsible for at Camp Fortune. Over the next two years 150 family passes were given to investors. But all good things eventually come to an end. The federal income tax department decided that the free passes given in lieu of interest were in fact income. Thus an almost painless form of funding dried up, but Camp Fortune, thanks in part to the efficient, improved operation of its uphill transportation systems, was enjoying a boom. Clifford and Saunders were doing well and the loans were all duly repaid.

During the early part of 1956 the NCC expressed an interest in purchasing the ski cabin John had built on Kingsmere Road. Various reasons were given. When it became apparent that their modest offers were not meeting with any success, the truth was forthcoming. The Park's administrators and planners wanted the cabin to be within the Park boundary. The NCC's offer was then sweetened so that John was unable to refuse. There was a charming 100-year-old house on the Meach Lake road, near the village of Old Chelsea, which John and Marg had noticed and admired many times on their way to the lake. If John agreed to sell the little cabin, they would temporarily rent them the Old Chelsea house while they made other living arrangements. John agreed, the deal was made, and John and family moved closer than ever to Camp Fortune.

John had always wanted to be as close to his work at Fortune as possible. His idea of being close was to be able to look out the kitchen window to see skiers ascending or descending. He wanted to literally keep his eye on the operation. Now that he was out of the little cabin on the outskirts of the Park, he arranged with the commission to purchase a suitable property in Camp Fortune Valley on which to build a house. Part of the agreement was that John would have to bring in the necessary power line at his own expense. The 1-mile long power line, as John designed it, not only provided his new home with power, but for the first time, it allowed the Ottawa Ski Club the possibility of electrical service as well.

Tragedy struck the Clifford family on the 16th of June 1957. The house in old Chelsea caught fire and burned to the ground; nothing was saved or salvaged. They lost all of their belongings; business records, all the trophies won in bygone days. John the optimist had very little insurance to cover the major loss. "I always thought that these things happened to the other guy." Eddy MacCabe, the Ottawa Journal's sports editor, wrote in his column that, "this was the first time that John and wife Marg were out of the house together and at the same time."

CHAPTER 15
White Gold

Snow, in its quantity and quality, often meant the difference between a successful and a disastrous skiing season. It was the uncontrollable factor. Ski areas could not always rely on a kindly providence; the shovel and attending manpower had to be called in. It was called "snow farming"; men shovelling the white gold out of the bush to the trail, hill or jump where it was needed.

Snow management was an important part of operating a ski area and could make the difference in the holding of a successful competition or even in remaining open at all. John, as a boy, had started his career helping fellow skiers' enjoyment of the sport with the Night Riders, cutting trails in the off-season, and servicing the trails of the OSC in winter, to keep them safe and passable. It was saw, machete and axe in the summer and fall, and shovel, shovel and more shovel most of the winter. As he matured, he helped solve the problem of uphill transportation by constructing and improving tows. He also built bigger and better ski-jumps. He was renowned as a consultant to the ski industry; regarded as one of its finest engineers. Whatever the accolades bestowed upon him, he could still be found, at one time or another, on the business-end of a shovel, heaving tons of snow out to where it would do the most good.

Each time he swung the shovel, his creative mind returned to the dream: "If there were only a way to make this stuff where and when we needed it." Guaranteed snow . . . snowmaking. It would be the magic lamp, the key to profitable operation.

An article in an American farming publication on irrigation caught John's eye in early 1956. On the theory that aerating sprayed water to create a mist might prevent frost damage in field crops, two gentlemen in the irrigation supply business had introduced a jet of compressed air into their rotary sprinkling nozzles. To their surprise, at certain temperatures, the device produced snow instead of water. Joe and Phil Tropiano, of Larchmont Farms, Lexington, Mass., had discovered the art of making snow.

Bill Walsh Jr. in upper New York State saw the same article. He took the idea and improved upon it with the creation of a more sophisticated nozzle that mixed two jets of compressed air with a single jet of water. He tested the unit at a local ski hill; it was crude but it worked. He patented the device, calling it the Skyworker Nozzle, and then sold the patent to the Tropiano brothers. They adapted the new nozzle to their portable, directional, irrigation gun, and patented the whole system as the Larchmont Snowmaking System.

John contacted the Tropianos, expressing interest in their snowmaking technique. They invited him to Lexington for a demonstration. Phil Tropiano told him that the gun would only produce snow when the temperature and humidity were within certain parameters: temperature had to be around -10 degrees Fahrenheit and not more than +20 degrees. The humidity could vary but was a concern at higher temperatures. John could hardly contain his enthusiasm. "My longest cross country drive to the western competitions seemed short in comparison to the lonely 300 miles I had to drive to Lexington . . . if it works . . . if . . . if . . . if!"

The conditions were perfect; his first view of snow making surpassed his most optimistic expectations. The water entered the gun at 50 gallons a minute, mixed with compressed air injected at 100 cubic feet per minute, and came out as a dense cloud of snow that settled across the field more than a hundred feet around the gun. He eagerly proposed an agreement for the Canadian rights. To his disappointment, the Tropianos did not immediately agree. They wanted time to decide if they were going to allow him the right to market their system in Canada.

John returned to Ottawa frustrated but undiscouraged. He was determined to bring snowmaking to Canada. He called the Tropianos repeatedly, but they continued to put him off. Just when the idea of patent infringement entered John's mind, they invited him to meet with them once again.

After a good deal of tantalizing small talk, they led him on a bit by showing him the many applications for rights that they had been deluged with. "At least," John said to himself, "they haven't had any other Canadian applications." Finally, they told him that they had weighed his track record of accomplishments; they liked him and felt he was the right man. The enthusiasm he had shown at their first meeting

The Larchmount snowmaking system operating on the Pee Wee hill at Camp Fortune.

had made its mark after all. The Tropianos granted him the Canadian marketing rights for the Larchmont System, and John had learned another lesson: You can't hurry a New Englander in a business deal.

The deal they put together was straightforward. John would import the American-made snowgun with its special couplings to be married with readily-available Canadian materials such as pumps, compressors and pipe fittings. In return the Tropianos would receive 50% of net Canadian profits for 10 years. With handshakes all around, John departed for Ottawa. His car was loaded with a "gun" and all the fittings that the car could hold.

It looked as if John was once again going to be sunk by the Federal Government when he reached the Canadian border. The Customs men were not easily convinced that the gun, with its tubular construction and tripod legs, was not in fact a weapon. Eventually he persuaded them that he was not intent on seizing control of the country by burying Ottawa in snow and he was on his way.

During the 1958 season, two years after reading of the unexpected emmission of snow from an irrigation gun, John and Steve Saunders completed their first snowmaking installation at Camp Fortune. The job initially looked straightforward, but with no experience to draw upon, they had to invent solutions to the numerous problems they encountered. Bill Walsh, the inventor of the Skyworker nozzle, visited Camp Fortune a few times giving them valuable advice. Ron Bailie, an engineer, and manager of Ingersoll Rand pump division, was also helpful in developing this first system. He went on to become the Toronto area distributor for Ingersoll but he never lost interest in John's projects lending his expertise and assistance in designing many future installations.

The completed snowmaking system was crude, but it worked. There was still some shoveling needed, but now it was only to add the finishing touch to the miracle. As John had foreseen, the word about snowmaking spread fast across Canada. Jake Robbins of Miller Paving installed a Skyworker System at the Don Valley Ski Centre in Toronto. It looked as if guaranteed snow was no longer an impossible dream. Man-made snow was going to be profitable for Clifford and Saunders, and, more significantly, John Clifford was supplying another tool to help assure that the Canadian ski industry would survive and prosper.

The Clifford and Saunders business was becoming a year-round operation. The volume of business had grown to a point where they needed more qualified help and were in a position to pay for it. They attracted skilled men such as Jeff White, a professional engineer who had just graduated from Carleton University, and Ralph Mallory, a local boy from Chelsea who was an excellent mechanic and field man, and Bill Vant,

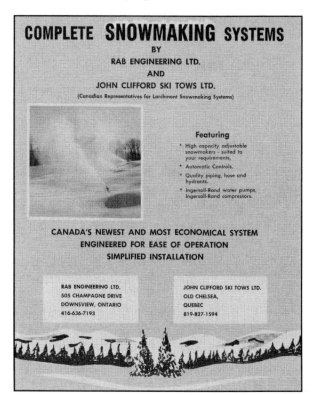

COMPLETE **SNOWMAKING** SYSTEMS
BY
RAB ENGINEERING LTD.
AND
JOHN CLIFFORD SKI TOWS LTD.
(Canadian Representatives for Larchmont Snowmaking Systems)

Featuring
* High capacity adjustable snowmakers - suited to your requirements.
* Automatic Controls.
* Quality piping, hose and hydrants.
* Ingersoll-Rand water pumps, Ingersoll-Rand compressors.

CANADA'S NEWEST AND MOST ECONOMICAL SYSTEM
ENGINEERED FOR EASE OF OPERATION
SIMPLIFIED INSTALLATION

RAB ENGINEERING LTD.
505 CHAMPAGNE DRIVE
DOWNSVIEW, ONTARIO
416-636-7193

JOHN CLIFFORD SKI TOWS LTD.
OLD CHELSEA,
QUEBEC
819-827-1594

a retired armed services Captain who became the firm's comptroller.

One after another contracts were signed. Every major ski area in Canada, over the next ten years, became a user of the Larchmont System, installed by John Clifford and company. All told they installed sixty-five systems across Canada. The Tropianos and their field man John Mathewson, on frequent trips to Canada to visit installations in progress, were always amused when they found their Canadian partner out on the hill swinging a shovel along with his men. They said they thought that the idea was to abandon the shovel altogether, not to give up shovelling snow for shovelling dirt.

Business continued to expand for Clifford and Saunders during 1958. Unfortunately, Steve's wife Helen became ill and her doctor prescribed a change of scene to aid her recovery. Steve offered to sell his share in the company to John so that they could do some travelling. Negotiations were completed in 1959, Clifford and Saunders was dissolved, and two new companies were formed with two new partners: Digby Veits, John's associate in the golf range project, and George Gowling, an executive with Ottawa radio station CFRA. Together they formed John Clifford Ski Tows Ltd. and Camp Fortune Ski Services Ltd. The Clifford and Saunders era was history.

A major job for the new company was the replacement of the landing hill of the Lockeburg jump. Constructed of wood only a few years before, it had collapsed under the weight of a very heavy snowfall in 1959. The club could not finance a replacement, and left the ruin where it lay until John decided to replace it in the summer of 1961. The city of Ottawa was eliminating electric street car service, scrapping the steel rails and poles. The rebuilt jump was going to resist any storm; John rebuilt it with the steel of the Ottawa Electric railway.

Using the new Franz Baier low-trajectory design, they completely reconstructed the jump, with a steel and concrete tower, a steeper landing, an uphill outrun, and a new judges' stand. The leftover rails were used to replace all of Camp Fortune's rotten wooden bridge stringers.

With such a magnificent jump available, John approached Georges Boivin, local sales manager for O'Keefe Brewery, asking him to convince the company to sponsor an annual O'Keefe Tournament of Champions, using the new jump as the venue. Pressing his luck, he further suggested they sponsor Canada's national Ski Team. He described how impressive the O'Keefe banner would look on the tower, backed up by another at the end of the outrun in sight of the thousands of spectators that would be drawn to the spectacle of the wingless flyers.

O'Keefe took him up on both suggestions after an inspection of the new facility. The Canadian team carried the O'Keefe name from 1961 through 1964 for an annual fee of $10,000.

The Tournament of Champions, sponsored by O'Keefe, was held at the Lockeburg site until 1979. Pleased that he had brought international recognition to Fortune, John remained in the background, leaving the running of the event to the many dedicated persons, competitors and administrators, who made the event a lasting success.

Noteworthy among these was Sigurd Lockeberg, the builder of the original jump that bore his name. He often contributed funds and helped organise many successful events. Russ Smart, Bob Wallace, Earl Pearlman, Art Levine, Ray Durocher, Odd Michaelson, Franz Baer, Colin Berg, Tor Wiebust, Georges Boivin, Fred Morris, Bill Petersen, Stig Sjolund, Réal Seguin and Paul and Jaques Bernique, all members of the Ottawa Ski Club, came forward with their help and expertise. They were the active few who kept jumping up with skiing's other disciplines.

Problems in operating the two corporations were as frequent as in any business, and generally dealt with as they arose. One problem, however, was not easily eliminated: during the 1959 season, someone was cutting the rope tows two or three times a week; particularily the Beamish hill tows and the tow on the gentle McHugh hill. A great deal of time was lost during the short ski day, resplicing sabotaged ropes.

Whoever the guilty party was, he was carefully covering his tracks. Eventually, they narrowed the field, speculating that the culprit might be a former volunteer worker, who having not been invited back, had lost his season tow ticket. The threat of arrest stopped him when they finally identified him. John managed to find somthing good in the situation: "With the abundance of practise forced on me, I became an expert in rope splicing. My splicing time went from over an hour to less than half. Find me a rope splicing competition; I'm sure I'd be a winner."

The 1950's and the 1960's were the fastest growth years of skiing. John had to keep a step ahead of the tidal wave of enthusiasts he was helping to create. He had to provide the facilities, the space, the on-hill environment to please the OSC member, the paying customer and the club executive. Aside from the ongoing demand for the best mechanical aids, he was aware of the need for higher, bigger-hill skiing. There were no hills available for development on the property suitable for training the club's up-and-coming racers. There were higher "mountains" just outside the club's boundaries; he needed a way to move a mountain to Camp Fortune, or, to move Fortune to the mountain.

Skyline Chairlift under construction. John, in sweater, supervising.

The OSC was unable to finance an opportunity that appeared in late 1958. A nearby higher property, the O'Reilly Estate was available. It was known as the Ski-Skule and had been developed by Bud Clark. It consisted of sixty-five steep acres, positioned horizontally across the mountain, affording only a short, fast downhill run. The National capital Commission owned a small strip of land at the bottom of the hill, and another strip or about twenty-five acres at the top, with O'Reilly's sandwiched in the middle.

John wanted to put the parcels together, providing the OSC with a hill with a 620 foot vertical drop, bettering the club's Cote du Nord by 320 feet. Assembling the package was not as simple as it looked. He believed his financial position was strong enough, but there were those who felt that he was making an investment decision for emotional rather than business reasons. As usual, John was ready to take any risk, emotional or otherwise, if it appeared to benefit Camp Fortune. He was not to be dissuaded.

After lengthy negotiations, John purchased the O'Reilly Esate through his company for $9,000. He promptly resold the property for $9,000 to the National Capital Commission, on the condition that the NCC join the two smaller pieces and lease the whole to the OSC for one dollar a year for twenty-five years. He renamed the hill Skyline Area, and the Ottawa Ski Club entered the big hill class.

John's graphic plans for Skyline development were accepted without challenge by the club's executive. His detailed presentation included the layout of trails and hills bearing the names Bud Clark, Percy Sparks, Anne Heggtveit and The Canadian. The hill would be serviced with the club's first 900-per-hour-capacity Poma lift. The development was to be Fortune's and Ottawa's glory, and another feather in John's cap.

The OSC raised the funds to cut the trails and to construct a summit clubhouse. The first season was successful beyond all expectation, prompting more devlopment for the coming season. The OSC invested a further $45,000 in Skyline improvements. John constructed a double chairlift, one of the first in Canada, at his own expense, to serve the expected thousands. Construction was complete for the late fall 1959 ceremonial opening. The Honorable George Hees, Oswald Parent, MNA for Hull, and Alan Hay, NCC Chairman cut the triple ribbon for the formal inauguration of the new chairlift.

Skyline Chairlift opening, 1960. Oswald Parent, MLA for Hull, Hon. George Hees, Allan Hay, NCC Chair, John Clifford.

The 1959-60 season was the year the Ottawa Ski Club became a world class area. Skyline was chosen as the site for the 1960 Canadian Championships, thanks to the efficient use of men and materials, good planning and a little politics. Governor General Georges Vanier accepted the invitation to present the trophies. During the festivities that followed, John was reminded of how he had carried the flag in South America, and now he was doing it once again, only this time at his beloved Camp Fortune.

The Sixties saw many new ski areas open across Canada. Each required a ski lift of one sort or another. In the days before tow hill skiing, a few hardy ski buffs would climb under their own power and used their remaining strength to ski back down. When up-hill towing became available the few became the many, expending all their energy on the descent. When the snow conditions were brought under control, even more skiers, hardy and otherwise, were out tearing up the hills. The thousands

Camp Fortune: Flextrack Nodwell groomers in foreground, Clifford home at left. Lockeburg jump top right.

became hundreds of thousands, all demanding the best of conditions, but none willing to boot pack the snow into place. Thus the art of mechanical hill grooming was born.

There were many contraptions put together in an attempt to simulate the effect of side stepping skis on powder snow. Forty-five gallon drums empty or full of water were hauled behind farm tractors, sometimes with disastrous results. Flexible metal screens, chains and wooden frames were hauled up lifts to be dragged down-hill by groups of skiers. The first tracked vehicles put into use had been designed for other purposes; they tore up the snow with their heavy treads. Some were adaptations of war surplus personnel carriers and some were modifications of Bombardier tracked overland taxis. Clearly, special equipment was necessary to do the job and there were engineering firms starting to develop such machinery.

"Three men from St. Cecile Masham started with me in the early '50's, snowshoeing and packing the slopes: Joe Phillippe; Aurele Faubert and Real Breton. They were invaluable in preparing the slopes before the grooming machines came on the market. We tried the Bombardier snow taxi, the Muskeg tractor and the Tucker Sno-cat, but none of them performed well. Not until we tried the the American-made Thiokol did machine grooming came of age." The Thiokol was not perfect but it was better than anything else that they had tried.

One of the first Canadian manufacturers of tracked units engineered expressly for hill grooming was the Flextrack Nodwell company. Flextrack had been manufacturing larger units for use in the Arctic. It was a short step for them to fabricate a vehicle suitable for ski areas. John answered their request for a Canadian distributor for the smaller version of their tundra tractors for the ski industry. By dynamically promoting the Flextrack; he was once again pioneering a technology that made skiing better for all concerned. The company was pleased to have him represent them, and Camp Fortune made an ideal showcase. John remembers Real and Aurele driving the hill-grooming tractors with their trusty snowshoes on the seat beside them.

John actively sought a dealership in any major item that would better the product offered by a ski area. In addition to Flextrack Nodwell, he represented, among others: Thiokol, Valley Engineering Grooming Attachments, Samson Lifts and Harusch Portable Handle Tows, Savio Poma lifts. There were more to come.

There was hardly a ski area of any consequence in all of Canada that was not equipped with something with Clifford's corporate name on it. The profits from these sales, which were at their peak in 1962 and 1963, enabled John to subsidize and service the area that, he felt, helped make it all possible; Camp Fortune and the OSC.

CHAPTER 16
Fortune and Carlington

In the 1958-59 Ottawa Ski Club year book, is an article entitled "SO YOU WANT TO BE A CHAMPION". The article explains John's philosophy of training and racing. More importantly, the article is prefaced by editor James S. Patrick's note that, in a few short lines, summarizes John Clifford's racing career. The note reads as follows: "John Clifford, the author of these random paragraphs, has probably won more ski competitions than anyone else in Canada and, until his home was burned in 1957, had a room full of trophies to prove it." The maturing John Clifford's name was not to be found as often on the race result pages as it was as the author of numerous informative and instructional articles.

His name was listed in the year book as a club director as far back as 1943. In the late 50's there is the occasional mention of John as "our property manager", which indeed he was from just about the time he built their first rope tow in the fall of 1945.

"They thought I was making a lot of money with my tow concession when they offered me an honorarium of only $500 to manage the club. I guess I must have thought so too when I accepted it."

In the 1961 OSC year book, John Clifford was for the first time referred to as Club manager. In that same publication there is an article that he wrote entitled "Economy Skiing - Camp Fortune Style." He wrote it to give a better understanding of the services which he was providing to the OSC and its members:

ECONOMY SKIING – CAMP FORTUNE STYLE

Do you know that there is no ski area in North America comparable in size to Camp Fortune that offers the facilities that the Ottawa Ski Club does for a low lift rate of $3.00 per day? To name a few areas and their charges:

	Per day
Toronto Ski Club at Collingwood	*$6.00*
Mont Gabriel	*$5.50*
Mont Tremblant	*$5.00*
Stowe, Vermont	*$6.50*

When the cost of your membership is pro-rated against the number of times you use the tow facilities, you will wonder how the ski club and the tow concessions can offer tow skiing at this low rate.

The Club and the Ski Tow Co. spend thousands of dollars each season to provide free instruction for children and the most complete competition programme in Canada. The Ottawa Ski Club is probably the only ski area on this contintent which supplies all round ski facilities to the low income person.

Many exciting improvements can be made at Camp Fortune in the future to benefit members, such as spacious lodges, improved cafeterias, etc. Also many of our gentle slopes such as Midget, McHugh, Morts and Paradise Valley can be made two times wider and their rope tows replaced by updated ski lifts.

Also, we hope to see paved roads to Camp Fortune, free parking on weekends, and good accommodation with the resort atmosphere. With the above mentioned additions the Ottawa Ski Club would have a ski recreational area fitting for the National Capital.

The following are some of the changes you will see at Camp Fortune this season:

A 900 per hour capacity Double Chair Lift which will operate year round on weekends and daily for the winter season, at the same rates as the T-Bars.

A 15' by 120' addition to the Skyline Lodge will ease the situation somewhat and parking for another 200 cars has been arranged with the Sparks family across the Meach Lake Road.

The sum of $22,000.00 was put into the widening and grooming of the R.P. Sparks Trail, the Bud Clark, and the Canadian. The Anne Heggtveit Slalom Hill, the finest slalom hill in Canada is useable, but needs a little more work. With the Double Chair Lift and recent grooming this Skyline Area can now handle 2000 skiers, and this on the minimum of snow. This is an amazing feat for a non-profit Club.

The Camp Fortune Valley itself has seen some major changes too. These include a concrete and steel artificial landing for the Sigurd Lockeberg Jump. This widened landing is the first stage of a 60 meter (220 ft.) hill designed by jumping Director Franz Baier. Future plans call for a short in-run tower of 38 feet in height, also a new judges' stand. This will be the only jump east of Sault Ste. Marie, Ontario capable of holding Jumping of International calibre. The $9,000.00 spent this summer includes 200 tons of concrete footing which combined with the steel rails will be an asset that will not rot away like the structures of the past.

Other improvements are additional parking for 400 cars, widening of the Alexander and Malcolm McDonald Hills, and repairs to bridges, lodges, etc.

Free parking on weekdays and night skiing 6 nights per week, excluding Sunday night, will be welcome to quite a few of the members.

I might mention a few facts about our Ski Tow Company. Actually there are two limited companies, John Clifford Ski Tows Ltd. and Camp Fortune Ski Services Ltd., the latter operating the Ski Shop managed by Reg Toomey with Peter Jessen handling the repair department, also, the Camp Fortune Ski School with Alex McDougall as director.

John Clifford Ski Tows Ltd. is entirely responsible for providing the tows and lifts, and the hill maintenance including the snow making installation which has been improved and will certainly get a work out this coming season, even if it's only to put down a base. We have provided a Viking type Chalet for our Assistant Manager/Accountant Dave Midgley so that when he is working those 18 hour days, he hasn't far to go to get home.

We will be providing daily ski condition reports with a Telephone Answering Service hook up. It is sometimes difficult to aim at a happy medium with these reports. As 60% of our membership are beginners we base the report on their requirements. "Poor" and "Fair" reports may still be *excellent skiing for the Expert and Intermediate skier. The Phone Number for this service is CE 9-9533, and it is listed under the Ottawa Ski Club in your Telephone Directory.*

We take great pleasure and pride in providing you with the best facilities at the lowest price, and we hope that you will always be proud to be an Ottawa ski Club member.

Fortune Valley: Skyline on left, Meech T-bar centre.

Obviously, he didn't run the place by himself. There were many dedicated volunteers who contributed to the growth and operation of Camp Fortune: Herb Marshall, a long-time president, Bill Ball, George McHugh, Elmer Cassel, Bill Irving, Harold Fawcett, Paul Lajoie, John Veit, Lucien Isabelle, Rolly Beaudry, Dave Wright, Ron Leafloor and Bernie Bureau. And all the volunteers who ran the races, the Night Riders, the schools and cafeterias, with Charlie Boland and his family.

How was it possible that Camp Fortune was able to offer its facilities for the lowest per day lift rate ($3.00 per day and $50.00 per season) of any major area in the east, in some cases at less than half that charged by others? With the huge expense of snow making and hill grooming, how was it possible for the Ottawa Ski Club to be the only major ski area supplying all-round, first quality ski facilities to the lower income skiing family? How was it possible that a non-profit club could build jumps, tee-bar lifts, double chairlifts, and still provide the attending personnel? It was because John Clifford was repaying a debt of gratitude by subsidizing Fortune's operations out of his other business revenues.

He freely offered himself and his personal service wherever he could. He did little more than cover his costs on any construction job done within the bounds of Fortune. As a concessionaire with the task of operating and maintaining the hills and tows, he was able to keep the costs down by not operating that segment of his business at a profit, and yet he paid 2% of gross for the rights to the concession. It was strange that no one wondered how he was able to give so much and charge so little.

John may have felt that he had a debt to pay to the OSC, but he was running a business and he had partners. His partners went along with him up to a point, but corporately profit was still the raison d'etre. Lift prices had not been increased for 13 years, and they knew that Fortune, despite having more lifts and services, charged the lowest price in all of Canada. John had to agree out of fairness to the business and his partners that it was time to increase the lift rates.

The partners agreed to ask the OSC executive for only a minimal increase for the services provided. The price increase was tempered to remain competitive with other eastern Canada areas. The increase in the lift rate was only $1.00, from $3.00 to $4.00 and this for adults only. The increase for the use of the rope tows was only 50 cents, from $1.50 to $2.00 and, with deference to the younger skier, and to John, the price was raised for adults only.

"To our complete disbelief the Club's directors refused our request. We asked that the issue be taken to arbitration. We won the arbitration but at great cost." This is the way John explains the first serious rift between himself and the Club's directors. Not wanting to drive the wedge in any further, he decided to leave the rates as they were, and he actually persuaded his partners to go along with him with the promise that he would "make up the difference.

The rates remained at the original low level for a few more years. This meant that John had to work harder at sales of snowmaking and grooming equipment to satisfy his partners and to keep the company in the black. The OSC was in fact being subsidized by Clifford Ski Tows Ltd.

With skiing was growing all over the country at a tremendous rate, Camp Fortune could not remain alone in the Gatineau area forever. Competition emerged just a few miles away; an area was opened by John's good friends, the Tommy brothers and Reg Lefebvre. Edelweiss was only 6 miles further than camp Fortune from Ottawa and would surely draw away some of Fortune's members. Their marketing strategy was designed to attract some of the business away from John's operation.

Edelweiss opened with a no membership fee promotion and they were only charging $2.50 for a lift ticket. John was concerned by the new competition, not just because they were so nearby, or because they were charging less for their lift: it was also the fact that his former partner, Steve Saunders supplied the lifts . . . and this perhaps with money that John was paying him as part of their buy-out deal. Arbitration or not, John was now compelled by this turn of events to leave Fortune's rates where they were.

Success often precipitates jealousy. Such was the case as Camp Fortune grew. Before John brought the club into the mechanized era, the club's membership was only 2500, comfortable for those who considered Fortune to be a private club, but certainly not enough to support the facilities that they wanted the club to have. As more hills were cleared, and more tows built, membership grew proportionately, tow line-ups became longer; five minute line-ups stretched to fifteen minutes or more. The lodges became more crowded, and according to some, John was making too much money.

The operations of snowmaking, hill grooming and lift maintenance didn't just happen. It took a lot of time, machinery and manpower to keep Fortune's slopes in the condition that the membership had become accustomed to. Efficiency was the key word, and John was having a tough time operating as he felt he should. The work that he had to accomplish every operating day was severely hampered because he did not have proper housing for the Thiokol groomers, no place to store parts, no shelter from the elements. He needed a garage.

He wanted to build an simple shelter at his own expense but the club's board of Directors refused him permission. These men were all very intelligent, they were professionals; lawyers, accountants, businessmen, all aware of profit and loss. John had easily proven the obvious need for the garage. Why refuse his request? John, used to accomplishing his goals under almost any conditions, assumed it was a decision made by men accustomed to a warm office environment; they were not the people who had to rid the equipment of accumulated snow and ice before it could be used; they just expected the hills to be in shape for the members.

Disappointed, he carried on maintaining the winter playground for the members and overseeing the operation of the club. Camp Fortune was now recognized as the largest ski club in North America, if not in the world at that time. Was John slow in

John Clifford Skitows equipment at Camp Fortune.

recognizing the beginning of the end of his Camp Fortune reign?

He was not concerned about being kicked out. The nature of his work, with the permanent installations that he had put in place and the support that he had from the membership at large led him into a false sense of security as far as his position at Camp Fortune was concerned. He did not recognize that there were other forces at work.

Still wishing to invest in the future of Ottawa skiing, John offered to install and operate ski facilities within the city at Carlington Park. He supposed that everyone involved would jump at the chance. After all, the shouts of happy children skiing down Carlington's gentle slope on a sunny winter's day should warm even a politician's heart.

When he explained that the new hill would produce thousands of new skiers, happy skiers that one day might become happy tax payers, the committee took the unprecedented step of granting John the project without going to tender. Lighthearted or not, the partnership still took a

Ronnie Stewart and Bob O'Billovich of the Ottawa Roughriders show off the team's ski trophy.

The Roughriders with their trophy after defeating the Ottawa media in their annual ski competition.

long time to arrange. There were members on Ottawa's council who were aware of the value of going into the ski business with a man with such a good track-record, but there were still a few that had to be convinced. Negotiations began in 1961, and were not completed until the spring of 1963. The hill would be named The Anne Heggtviet Hill.

The site, on the north side of the Carlington Reservoir in the City's west end, opened with a 600-foot long and 400-foot wide, smooth slope, served by a T-bar capable of moving 1400 skiers every hour. The golf-course-smooth hill had snowmaking equipment to add to whatever the weather produced and bright arc lights for evening skiing.

Including the time that it took John to sell the idea, it had taken over four years to complete a project that should have taken less than a year. Aside from the council

Summer activities: the riding centre gave lessons to more than one hundred students every Saturday. John organized gymkhanas, events and trail rides.

members that needed persuasion, the project was almost killed at the signing stage when Mayor Charlotte Whitton, the same lady that dealt the death blow to the Rockcliffe jump project, stepped into the picture. The council had signed the agreement to go ahead when she was away on vacation. The Mayor was adamant that the project be put on hold even though John Clifford's company was prepared to put up over $40,000 to the city's $18,000. She insisted that the project go to tender. It did, but no one else was interested in submitting a tender. At long last the project was allowed to proceed.

On the 15th of December 1965, newly-elected Mayor Don Reid cut the ribbon that formally opened the hill. John still wonders if Mayor Whitton might have been there to cut the ribbon if she not generated all the negative publicity with its consequences at the polls. "We ran into a lot of roadblocks along the way," he mused, shortly before

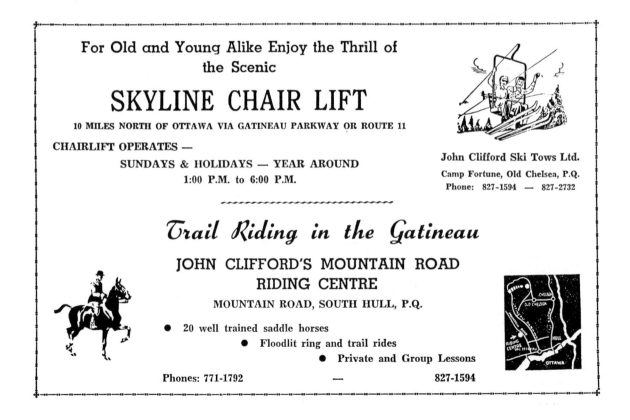

leaving on a business trip to Switzerland that kept him away from the opening ceremonies. He missed the opening fireworks at the park, but he had a ten-year contract with the city to prove his idea's worth.

The line of continuity in the development of Camp Fortune and the operation of the Carlington Park facility never ceased during those busy years. As Fortune and skiing grew, so did John. His horizons were expanding. He needed another goal; Carlington Park was a stepping stone; it provided another farm system to get more youngsters, the future market, on skis,. Because of the Kiwanis programs, which were generating thousands of enthusiastic skiers, demand was growing rapidly for new facilities and more challenging skiing. It was now time to start the next step in his overall plan to establish the Gatineau area as a destination area for the people of greater Ottawa and Hull, and for the country as a whole.

"There is a sort of natural evolution in the skier," John would tell anyone interested. "As they conquer one slope, they progress to a more difficult one, and eventually they begin to cast about farther afield as local areas fail to satisfy them." His philosophy ran parallel to the skiers' evolution. It was a natural step for him to want to provide bigger and better ski areas for his skiers.

John knew where to go to create the ski area of his dreams; Mont Ste. Marie whose majestic beauty he had first seen from a canoe on his many trips in younger days. The mountain, only 60 miles north of Ottawa, had only Mont Tremblant in the Laurentians, more than a hundred miles away, as the crow flies, as competition. How could he miss? The plans for the mountain had been on the drawing board of his mind for more than 12 years. The timing was right; he had another mountain to conquer.

CHAPTER 17
Mont Ste. Marie

John started investigating Mont Ste. Marie's potential in 1958; he and Russ Smart made an annual expedition for the purpose. They studied the mountain from all sides. He enjoyed inviting others along to enjoy and explore the mountain with him. Reg Toomey and Ham Quain remarked, "He showed us the mountain as if he owned it. We didn't doubt for a minute that this man would someday own it and develop it."

By the winter of 1961/62 exploration of the mountain had progressed to the point where it was time to plan where the lifts would be placed and where the downhill runs would be cut. John secured the services of the well-known aerial photographer, Alex O'Nosko. Chartering an aircraft with an experienced mountain pilot, they took pictures of the mountain from every angle. Plans were now coming together; with notes taken over the years and photos spread out over every flat surface in his house, the proposed lift lines and trails were drawn. Mont Ste. Marie was taking shape on paper and starting to look like a world class ski development. With the plans in place the next step would be the attempt to purchase the land . . . the mountain.

Extreme care had to be taken in order that John not be recognized for the potential developer that he was. If word got out that he was buying for development, prices might climb. Frank McIntyre, an experienced Gatineau real estate agent, assured John that he would be able to acquire options on some of the farms around the base of the mountain without raising any suspicion. McIntyre proved to be the expert that he claimed to be; within a few days he acquired options to purchase 5 strategically located farms.

Now it was John's turn. Although they were very careful not to let the cat out of the bag, there was still a lot of money involved, more money than John had. Ever the optimist, and armed with lengthy options that allowed adequate time, he believed he was in a good position. All he had to do was sell the idea to his bankers. He had to take his time preparing his financing request, backing it up with full documentaion. He was determined to create a presentation that would be impossible to refuse. No one else was was looking at the mountain as he was; time was on his side . . . he thought.

The mountain had been quietly sitting there in the Gatineau region, surrounded by pristine lakes and rivers, minding its own business since creation. A few hardy farmers had occupied its lower flanks but generally speaking it was uninhabited. When John started to explore it for eventual commercial development there were only a few hiking trails leading to campers' cottages and logging sites. Roads out of nearby Ryanville, situated on the mountain's west side, were rough, often impassible. It seemed that the mountain would maintain its serene isolation for eons to come.

The founders of Club Mont Ste. Marie: Rear: Reg Toomey, Russ Smart, Guy Laframboise, Frank McIntyre. Front: Don Bohart, Al Wotherspoon, John Clifford, Harold Fawcett, Marcel Joyal

However, this was the cold war era. North America, according to the military strategists of the time, had to protect itself from sneak attacks from the north. The Department of National Defense chose the top of the mountain as a site for a "gap filler" radar station. John and his realtor had just obtained the options on the five farms when the first gravel pits were opened at the mountain's base. In no time at all, construction was underway and a road to the summit was built.

John found it incredible that another of his ventures was to be complicated by political intrusion. "If I wanted to develop this mountain I had to move fast or surely, with the increased traffic, someone else would discover its potential." John immediately mounted another expedition, only this time it was to sell his brainchild to investors.

Choosing a warm, sunny day, John and Russ Smart brought potential investors Brian O'Brien, Marcel Joyal and Wally White out to the mountain. "We climbed part way up the gentler slopes in snow over two feet deep," recalls John. "Powder snow . . . up to our knees . . . couldn't have arranged it better." By the time the party arrived back in Ottawa they had agreed that the development of the mountain was a worthwhile venture.

A plan was quickly formulated to raise $30,000 from 30 people who would gaurantee $1000 each. This group would thereafter be known as the Group of Thirty. In return, the corporation that John was to set up would give each of the founding group a half acre lot and a lifetime family season pass. These passes, reflecting the faith that John had in the project, would remain valid until the year 2000. This arrangement made it possible for John to immediately borrow the $30,000 from the bank, in order to exercise the options on the five farms that he possessed.

As a consequence, more land around the base of the mountain became available. Other landowners, who had at first been skeptical, saw that options indeed had been taken up. John was once again strapped for cash to take up new offers, but he did not let the potential vendors know it. Assuring them that sales would be completed as soon as the papers were drawn up, he entered into phase two of the Mont Ste. Marie financing.

The Group of Thirty idea had worked, so he tried it again, only this time it was a group of 10 who were offered the same deal. With this money, John took up the latest offers. He now owned the lower reaches of the mountain; all he needed was the top half to complete the parcel.

While John was assembling the lower parcel, the Federal Government was busy building the radar station, including the valuable two mile long access road that led to the station and the summit. After tense negotiations the Defense Department eventually welcomed John's project. As it turned out, the radar base became obsolete within three years of its construction; the government put the facilities up for sale and John's bid of $6,500 was the highest. He became the owner of the facility, including the road to the top. All that was left to complete the package was the acquisition of the remaining land that was virtually the top half of the mountain, owned by the province of Quebec.

Mont Ste. Marie: the radar station at the summit, upper left; 1250 foot vertical drop, Cote Vanier on right.

Negotiations for the Quebec-owned portion of the mountain were the most difficult part of the deal. The early stages narrowed down to an offer to purchase 1200 acres, through John's Gatineau Member of Parliament, Mr. Roy Fournier. They were up against powerful opposition from the lumber companies who held timber rights on the acreage. But John had faced formidable opponents before.

After many fruitless trips to Quebec City, John decided that he was getting nowhere in the morass of lower bureaucracy; he had to go to the top. "The top" turned out to be the same gentleman, who, as Federal Minister of Transport, had cancelled his waterski school permit years before: Jean Lesage, now Premier of Quebec. At the time, John believed the Minister genuinely regretted that the permit had to be revoked: "He told me how sorry he was . . . and that perhaps someday he would be able to do something to make up for it." That day had arrived.

Lesage remembered him. John's lawyer of many years, Hamilton Quain, and his father and brother, Redmond Sr. and Redmond Jr. helped with negotiations. A deal was worked out: John would buy out the lumber companys' rights for $30 an acre, and purchase the 1200 acres for another $30 an acre. At least another $400,000 in improvements was to be invested into the property. An order -in-council gave John the option to buy the rest of the mountain. The only remaining question was, as he put it, "How the hell to do it ?"

The Autumn of 1965 was more colourful than usual. Mont Ste. Marie put on a show to welcome her potential owner. John climbed the mountain more often than ever, just to enjoy the blessings that mother nature had endowed upon her slopes . . . and to dream. The colours were spectacular; reds, oranges, shades of gold and green all blending into nature's finest collage. But it was not autumn's colours that filled his senses; he envisioned the slopes of white, outlined by the deep green of firs, that were to provide the best skiing west of Tremblant and east of the Rockies. Darkening his dreams was the frightening possibility that he would be unable to raise the remaining money to complete the mountain's purchase.

While negotiating with Quebec, John had been spreading the word that more funds might be needed and he was concerned about the resistance that was surfacing. In further consultation with Russ Smart he came up with the idea that should Quebec's price be too high to handle, another plan should be ready and waiting in the wings. They did not have to create plan "B". It came to them unsolicited.

The skiing business world was becoming nervously aware of the Power Corporation's entry into the field. The Company, under the banner of Holiday Resorts

John with Power Corp's Harold Milavsky at Grouse Mountain in B.C.

Limited, with President Jim Scott, and Treasurer Harold Mahlavski, was moving aggressively into the ski area market. They had already purchased the Chantecler Lodge at Ste. Adele Quebec and had options on Mont Tremblant. In the west they had purchased 55% of Sunshine near Banff, and the Voyageur Inn, also in Banff. Their purchases further west on the B.C. coast included control of Whistler's Mount Garibaldi and the Hot Springs Hotel in Terrace.

Aware of John's activities in the development of Mont Ste. Marie, Holiday Resorts sought him out, and made him two offers. First, they would be willing to invest $600,000 in Mont Ste. Marie in return for a 55% share. Of course this offer was the immediate answer to his financial problem; but 55%?

The second proposal was that he act as their consultant and look over the gondola lift construction which was just getting underway on the west coast at Whistler Mountain. Although he had only two weeks to accept the principal proposal, he put aside the offer to purchase and jumped at this opportunity.

They seemed to understand his reluctance to give an immediate answer to their financing proposal, and welcomed his acceptance of the consultancy position. Reminding him that he had plenty of time to consider the $600,000 offer, they suggested that he pack his bags for immediate departure for the west.

Pressure was beginning to mount. The Group of Thirty and the Group of Ten were quite apprehensive. Why was there no movement on the project? Were the promised crowds of skiers only figments of John's over-active imagination? The tension of keeping his investors mollified and the impossibility of getting Quebec to move without guaranteed financing was keeping John on edge. The Power

Corporation's offer to buy controlling interest, assuring Mont Ste. Marie's completion, looked good, as did the opportunity to get out of town for a while.

"I hardly had time to pack before a limousine arrived at my door to take me to the airport. As soon as I had agreed to look at their gondola installation, I was whisked off. Were they afraid that I might change my mind?"

At Whistler, he was taken in hand by Mr. Franz Williamson, President and General manager of the area. "He was constantly at my side," John recalls. "Mr. Williamson and his cronies made me feel very important." They flew him about in the corporate helicopter, all the while asking his advice, picking his brains. Without a moment to himself, one day led swiftly into the next; meetings and consultations were taking up every available minute.

The attention was overwhelming. During one of the frequent helicopter survey flights, John was snapped out of the complacency which had overtaken him when he saw the new lift towers creeping up the mountain. That was what he wanted to see back east and there were only a few days left before he had to accept or reject the Power Corp's offer. An alarm went off in his head; was this the real reason that he was being kept so busy? He was using up the option time that had been attached to their offer, time that could be more usefully spent seeking other avenues of financing his Mont Ste. Marie. John was learning about some of the subtle ways of big business.

Decisions in downhill racing are made in fractions of a second. Experienced racers like John could alter course and adjust to the unexpected in split-seconds. On this unfamiliar course, he realized that he had to make an adjustment at once or he would be out of time, with no choice but to accept Power Corp's offer.

There was another that was not as yet in writing. Mrs. Vera Stepan, a lady whom John had met the summer before when he was considering the feasibility of purchasing Mont Ste. Marie, had at the time suggested that he meet with the president of the international corporation, based in Switzerland, that she represented. He had purchased a cottage property on Lake Pemichangan, just beyond Mont Ste. Marie.

In Mrs. Stepan's Ottawa office, John met Mr. Dieter Bührle, the major shareholder of Bührle Holding Ltd., better known as Oerlikon of Switzerland. John offered him a 50% interest if he would make a substantial investment in the Mont Ste. Marie development. Bührle, agreeing that the potential was there, countered with an offer for 51%, saying, "John, accept my offer and you will never regret it." Without committing himself, John came away from that meeting considering Bührle's offer his ace in the hole.

Bührle's offer had been made over a year ago; was it still on the table? John had no excuse for his procrastination in getting back to Bührle. With so little time left he had to get home as quickly as possible to see if the Swiss connection was still alive. Telling Williamson that there was little else that he could do for them at the moment, he asked to be excused. Try as he might, Mr. Williamson could not hold onto him any longer.

When John had accepted the position of consultant to the Power Corp., he had left the completion of the Carlington Park area in capable hands within the Clifford Ski Tow Company; his men were qualified and experienced, so that was the least of his worries as he headed west. Succumbing to an offer that would have left him with only 45% ownership in Mont Ste. Marie was the real worry.

Back in Ottawa, John got in touch with Mrs. Stepan. Assuring him that he was doing the right thing in not accepting the Power Corp's. proposition, she arranged for an immediate telephone meeting with Mr. Bührle in Zurich. During the long-distance negotiations, Bührle sweetened his input to $750,000, in return for the 51% ownership; John would retain the remaining 49%. John felt secure in his minority position because he would be there to run things. The fact that he was Canadian also gave him a sense of security. He was going to see his mountain developed just as he had visualized in his mind's eye for so many a years. All that remained was a trip to Switzerland and the signing.

He had to excuse himself from attending the opening of the Carlington Ski Center. The flight to Switzerland was one of the most enjoyable that he had ever taken. His first class ticket was provided by Mrs. Stepan. John wondered if Bührle numbered Swissair among his corporate holdings.

With the paperwork completed and the financing in place, the deal was closed. His partner's hospitality in Zurich was luxurious. He had the finest accommodations and had been taken to the best restaurants, including more than one of Bührle's private clubs. The royal treatment, once again, this time on the other side of the Atlantic.

He flew back to Ottawa with Bührle's parting words, "You won't be sorry John," repeating over and over in his head, feeling apprehensive. It had been a close call, almost signing with the wrong party. The agreement signed that day, December 16, 1965, may not have been a momentous day for the Swiss, but to John, the business man-skier, it was like winning the first part of a combined: he still had to negotiate the twists and turns of the mountain's physical development; a larger project than he had ever undertaken before.

With the major hurdles overcome, the huge development was under way. The plans called for Mont Ste. Marie to develop in three stages, the $600,000 first stage being Ryan's Peak, emphasizing beginner and intermediate skiing, a 4,700-foot double chair-lift, a 1,100-foot beginner's chair-lift, 4 miles of down-hill trails, 2 miles of "Radar Road" for beginners; parking for 1,000 cars and of course, snowmaking. Stages two and three would include more expert runs and the construction of luxurious base lodge facilities.

Wood cutting on the first major trails began in January 1965, just weeks after John returned from Switzerland. The plans called for that part of the job to be complete by the coming spring, with construction progressing very quickly towards an opening the next December. How smoothly things progressed with adequate funding!

The Ottawa Citizen ran a small ad that summer: "Attention male students 16 years and over. Earn a season pass working Saturdays, September 20 to November 15 – Telephone for details." Clifford was up to his old tricks; the young men came in droves.

One early September afternoon John took a party of newspaper, radio and television reporters on a walking tour over the developed portion of the mountain. He could only show them stage one of the three-part plan but they were aware that they were being shown the best that Clifford had ever produced. That afternoon John announced the opening date, December 10, 1966. By opening day, John figured that he would have spent about $400,000. He was bringing his flagship in under budget. Feeling very optimistic, John was sure that this would please and impress his many partners.

Conditions were anything but ideal for the official opening of Mont Ste. Marie. The downpour failed to dampen John Clifford's enthusiasm when Gabriel Loubier, Quebec Minister of Tourism, Fish and Game, snipped the soggy ribbon symbolically suspended between a pair of ski poles.

Also present at the official opening, just as wet but equally enthusiastic, were Roy Fournier, Gatineau MNA and Gilbert de Dardel, Charge d'Affairs at the Swiss Embassy. Other officials at the ceremony included George Schmidt, Secretary of the Swiss Embassy and Mayors of the surrounding towns; Marcel D'Amour of Hull, Don Britt of Maniwaki, Rejean Lafreniere of Lac Ste. Marie, Jack Noonan of Low, Fernand Perriard of Kazabazua, and Daniel Rochon of Gracefield.

Phase one of the three-stage development plan had been completed. If everything went as scheduled, phases two and three were to be realized by 1970. An ironic footnote to the ceremony was that the official opening was also the official closing. John announced that they could not open for skiing that day, due to the inclement weather.

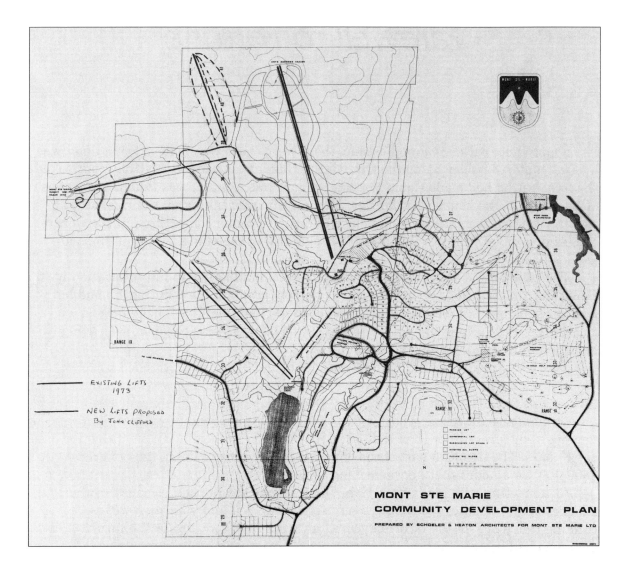

CHAPTER 18
Farewell to Fortune

Meanwhile, back at Camp Fortune, there were those who believed that John was making a pile of money using the Ottawa Ski Club as a springboard. They overlooked the fact that he had made Camp Fortune what it was, that he was the man who was on the hook at the banks, that he was the man who was taking all the risks, that he was the competitive skier who had placed Fortune's young competitors in the world's eye. And now, with the opening of Mont Ste. Marie in the offing, a few, perhaps a jealous fringe, wanted John and his "lucrative" concessions out.

The campaign of provocation designed to get John to give up his association with Camp Fortune fell on deaf ears. John was fiercely proud of the fact that he had built Fortune's membership to more than 15,000 skiers, making it by far the largest ski club in the world. He would not be driven out. If he was going to go, he was going to be bought out, and for a substantial sum.

The harassment changed to a buy-out offer in 1971. A committee led by President Vic Allen and Vice President Wy Lawson, suggested that if John would sell his concessions to the Ottawa Ski Club, they would keep him on as manager but under newer, more specific terms. They suggested that his management contract be changed to a one year term rather than the ten years that was in force, with an option for nine more years. The financial part of the offer was interesting to John; they offered $500,000, an amount that he was willing to entertain.

At a meeting with his lawyer, Ham Quain, he decided to sell. The cash value was adequate and the assurance of the committee that, "You and your men will be running this place for the next ten years," answered his concern for the future of his men who had been so faithful over the years. The decision became even easier for

98

John Clifford Skitows at the Central Canada Exhibition, Ottawa: John Irvin with instructor John Hanna on the ski deck.

John when Quain said to him "You'll still be running the place and you won't have to worry about the Club's financial situation. If they want to raise prices, the membership will not be able to fault you." Even though he still had 14 years to run on his contract with the Club, he heeded his attorney's advice.

The agreement read in part that the OSC would take over most of the Clifford Ski Tow's employees, leaving six men who would work at the Club, which would pay John $33,000 for their services. That would cover about half their annual salaries. John would have the use of these men in his other enterprises if they were not needed by the Club. He himself would be kept on as manager at $1000 per month, providing that he would attend all of their meetings and lend assistance where needed. He was also assured that the Club would stop trying to break the ten-year lease that he had on his house on Camp Fortune property. It was also suggested that the agreement be consummated as quickly as possible, as the Federal government had declared that after January 1, 1972, a capital gains tax would come into effect on any business sold after that date. Although its terms indicated a contrary intention, the agreement John signed in good faith signalled the end of the Clifford era at Camp Fortune.

The OSC executive, far from fulfilling the expectation of John's continued management implicit in the agreement, had within ten days of the signing hired a former employee of John's as the new manager, limiting John's responsibilities to attendance at operating meetings. Other actions and threats of actions calculated to provoke and embarrass John both personally and financially made it clear to him that any further influence he might try to exert at Camp Fortune would only be at the expense of bitterness, strife and probably legal dispute – unprofitable to the parties involved, and definitely damaging to skiing in the area. The Club insisted that the

John Clifford Ski Tows exhibit at the Central Canada Exhibition, promoting Mont Ste. Marie, Camp Fortune and Carlington.

spare parts for all the tracked vehicles and snowmaking equipment in John's inventory were theirs and that he had to pay for them.

There were many OSC members who were incensed by the treatment their executive had given to the man that they considered to be Mr. Fortune. They were also aggravated by the substantial rise in membership fees, tow rates and parking charges that they were suddenly subjected to. Membership dwindled rapidly. Wasn't this exactly what the private club types wanted? Wy Lawson was Vice President at the time and he fully expected to be the Club's next President. To no one's surprise Lawson did not receive the Club's vote for the top position.

Mr. Ross Walker became the next President. With Lawson voted out the members had shown their displeasure with the handling of the Clifford affair. The Ottawa Ski Club enjoyed a membership of 15,000 plus at December 28, 1971. The membership at the time that John stepped in with his borrowed $500 in 1945 was only 2500. It was never to increase again, and John sadly predicted, should the OSC not change its ways, it faced eventual extinction.

CHAPTER 19
Trouble at Mont Ste. Marie

After the gala Opening in December of 1966, everything proceeded as planned for the development of Mont Ste. Marie as a destination resort. The plans called for an Alpine Village of independantly owned inns, motels and restaurants, similar to most destination resorts in North America.

On March 11, 1966, John had signed an agreement with Oerlikon-Bührle Holdings, engaging him as President and Chief Executive Officer of Mont Ste. Marie Limited at a salary of $10,000 per year. In June of 1967, he was informed in a letter that Mr. Gary Clarke, son-in-law of Oerlikon's Canadian Comptroller, Vera Stepan, was appointed Executive Vice-President and Comptroller, and John's friend Russell Smart was to be Chairman of the Board. While Mr. Bührle was sitting behind his big mahogany desk in Zurich telling John he wouldn't regret becoming his partner, Gary Clarke was attending one of the world's best business schools in Lauzanne, Switzerland.

All future communication between John and the company was to be in writing to either Gary Clarke or Hans Reichsteiner, the Swiss Comptroller of Oerlikon. Over the next two months more than 100 letters, telegrams and memos changed hands, as John attempted to persuade his Swiss partners that his plan was the viable one. Helping John with the flood of correspondence was his legal advisor Hamilton Quain and the comptroller of John's own companies, Bill Vant.

During this time John continued with development of the mountain, including the design of the subdivision streets and the installation of the underground water system, with the help of employees Jeff White, Ralph Mallory, Reg Toomey, John Hanna and others.

Invitational downhill race on Radar Road, Mont Ste. Marie. Skiers are being towed by a Thiokol vehicle.

In April of 1965, as part of the original arrangement, John had agreed to transfer to M.S.M. Ltd. his options for all rights to the Quebec government lands he had acquired, including the buildings, radar tower and the two mile road to the top of the mountain. In June, 1967 Hans Reichsteiner informed him by telegram that Oerlikon wished to do all the financing internally, rather than from Canadian sources, and requested that John pledge his shares as security to the parent company. John refused.

On August 8, 1967 John wrote to Dieter Bührle and his sister Hortense Anba, explaining the difficulties he has been facing. His letter was returned on September 11, with an offer of a six month option to purchase their shares in M.S.M. Ltd. for $600,000. He approached the Federal Business Development Bank for financing, but, being unfamiliar with the financial viability of the kind of development John was doing, they turned him down.

On December 15, 1968, M.S.M. Ltd. offered to sell John all tows, buildings, machinery and a 50 year concession for $225,0000 covered by a security mortgage on the assets. John's new company, Mont Ste. Marie Ski Lifts Ltd. eventually had to borrow a further $200,000 from M.S.M. Ltd. to install the Cheval Blanc Chaiirlift.

John had erected a chalet at the base of the mountain during the initial phase of Mont Ste. Marie's construction so that he could be on the site 24 hours a day. The house was not at all pretentious, but it was well placed for its intended purpose as construction office and home. Most important was the view that John had of the mountain from his window. Nothing could escape his watchful eye; when the mountain opened for business he was able to watch the coming and going of his skiing customers; he could observe the length of the lift line and the descent of the skiers on the lower slopes, and at the same time, evaluate the condition of the snow.

First came the surveyors who busied themselves staking out a large area between John's house and the base of the ski slope. John did not have to be a mind reader to realize what was happening; Gary Clarke was about to build a huge chalet.

He hoped it was going to serve the same useful purpose for the new management as the house that he now occupied. Unfortunately, the new building turned out to be a private residence for Mr. Bührle whenever he came for a visit.

Another important part of John's master plan called for further subdivisions and the sale of land around the base of the mountain to supporting interests like hotels, motels, restaurants and shops. Mont Ste. Marie was a long 55 miles from Ottawa and Hull. The distance over poor roads made a day trip very long and arduous. Hotel accomodations were absolutely essential, but it did not seem that Oerlikon was going to follow the original plan. They wanted no part of other entrepreneurs getting in. Their plan was to build a major hotel and conference centre sometime in the future and have any services provided by concessionaires. Oerlikon was very slow in providing anything resembling sound growth; the area had been in operation for seven years, and still there were no significant provisions for overnight sleeping accommodation for those who wanted to spend more time skiing and less on the road. It was still a case of finding a scarce room in one of the nearby villages or returning home.

John was afraid that the momentum that the business was enjoying would falter if accommodations were not provided. Feeling that any further delay would be harmful, John and Fritz Dubach, a former Camp Fortune Ski Patroller, decided to go into the motel business. John would remain in the background while they found a way to provide inexpensive accommodation. The answer was in montreal. Thousands of temporary motel units had been built for Expo 67. They were being sold off for $1,000 each, completely outfitted. They bought 16 units and had them installed at Mont Ste. Marie. They were by no means luxurious but they were far better than the rough open-sided lean-tos that John had slept in on Mount Washington in his early days. The provision of accomodation met the province's liquor license requiremnts, and so Mont Ste. Marie's application for a permit was at long last approved.

John sold a small piece of property, at the edge of the ski area's parking lot, to

John with trout from his lake at Mont Ste. Marie.

Mr. and Mrs. Hector Stephanie, experienced gourmet restaurateurs. They built a small restaurant called "Piscadou". As John had foreseen, the skiers patronised the restaurant for lunch, and many stayed for an aprés-ski dinner. The 16 motel units and the Piscadou were not exactly on the scale John had envisioned; however, the basic goal of providing peripheral services to skiers to enhance the mountain's attractions was being accomplished.

Without question, if the ski development was to continue to prosper and grow, larger more luxurious accommodations would have to be put in place as promised.

John had felt very secure in his choice between the original bidders for his hand in the development of Mont Ste. Marie. He chose the Swiss over the Power Corporation because he figured that they, being a foreign company, would trust his Canadian expertise, that they would be more likely to keep out of his hair.

He knew that Mr. Dieter Bührle

was the head of the largest family-owned private business in the world, Oerlikon. The money that was lent to Lac Ste. Marie Lifts Ltd., John's company, was guaranteed by Oerlikon. John in turn gave his expertise and more importantly the land that he had purchased with the help of the Group of Thirty, as collateral.

The development was receiving a great deal of publicity, usually headlining John Clifford as the owner-developer. This made good sense, as John's name gave credibility to the project. But as the ski development grew in popularity, the papers printed more and more corrections and retractions which stated that John was not the owner-developer, that he was only the lift concessionaire.

Mont Ste. Marie in 1967: New lodge under construction, Thiokol groomer in foreground.

It was obvious by this time that Oerlikon wanted to take over, and rather than getting into a profitless war, John decided to sell out during the summer of 1974. The final price was $400,000 and included the surrender of his private lake on the back of the mountain. John called Finance Minister John Turner, who was in charge of the Foreign Investment Review Agency for permission to sell the business to oa foreign owner. Turner had previously agreed to loan the Quebec Government 1.8 million dollars to upgrade the access roads into Mont. Ste. Marie and Mont casades.

Soon after the negotiations were completed, the construction of the long-awaited hotel began. It was to be a grandiose structure, the likes of which had never before been seen at any ski resort in Canada. The sixteen motel units were moved to the site and used for staff quarters. Bottomless funding saw the building completed in record time. The hotel included all the amenities that $12,000,000 could buy. But Oerlikon had forgotten that the real reason for the hotel's existence, its bread and butter, was to provide accommodation for skiers. Anything else would be gravy. If the skiers were happy, with proper marketing to attract them from beyond Ottawa, the hotel could be kept full. Mont Ste. Marie would become a destination resort if the ski facilities were first rate. The Swiss reversed this philosophy. Their hotel, located 55 miles from Ottawa, was to be a conference center, the main attraction; the skiing was to be an extra. With this strategy in mind, the mountain's development was curtailed.

The little restaurant on the edge of the parking lot that had become so popular was forced to close. The high cost of skier accommodations made it possible for only the wealthy few to stay over in the new hotel. The resort's policy was not designed to take care of the day skier, the backbone of the industry. The daily and season ticket prices were raised to try to cover the loss of skier-visit revenue that resulted. It was not only time-consuming to get to Mont Ste. Marie, it had become expensive as well.

The loyalty of skiers, to both the operator and the area, demonstrated by the diminishing skier visits after John departed, was something else that was overlooked; Mont Ste. Marie's owners were losing a lot of money.

CHAPTER 20
Mont Cascades

When John was building his house at Camp Fortune, he purchased the lumber from Milton Cross, the owner of several retail lumber yards. Mr. Cross also owned lumber tracts and a saw mill along the east side of the Gatineau River. Included in the acreage that Mr. Cross owned was a mountain known as Mont Cascades. It was only 12 miles as the crow flies from Ottawa, but isolated, as it was only accessible by impassible logging trails. He asked John if he would, in his spare time, look at the mountain to assess the feasibility of turning it into a ski resort. Even though Mont Ste. Marie was his prime focus, John agreed, saying that when it was for the growth of skiing, he would somehow manage to fit it in.

The year was 1970. The pressure at Mont Ste. Marie was taking its toll on John so he actually welcomed the "business trips" that he took to look over Mont Cascades for Milton Cross. Most of the explorations were made in the winter and John was once again in the bush, where he was able to forget the everyday problems of operating a business. This, he had to admit to himself, was what he really liked the most, on snowshoes or cross-country skis, by himself, exploring virgin territory.

He explored every inch of Mont Cascades. He remembers that winter with mixed feelings; on one hand, the complete freedom that only snow and skiing could give him and the other, the reality of Mont Ste. Marie. When he gave Mr. Cross his report in the spring of 1971, he was sure that the potential was there, but only with the construction of a proper access road. Cross prevailed upon John, with his expertise, to approach the Quebec government to see if they would put in the road that would make the project possible. John agreed, and met with Mr. Roy Fournier, MNA for the

Gatineau area. John was not happy about courting a politician again, but the feeling of being in the starting gate of another race was exhilarating.

The meeting was a classic Clifford presentation, resulting in an agreement on John's part to start building another major ski resort in Quebec as soon as the road construction to Mont Cascades commenced. Cascades would start off with the construction of not one but three lifts. John had given his word and Fournier was confident that the commitment would be honoured. It was an offer that Mr. Fournier felt he could not refuse.

Mont Cascades: chairlift under construction, Bob Gratton with John, holding plans.

"Three lifts, Mr. Clifford; that sounds very substantial to me," Fournier said as John was leaving. His constituents would love to see Clifford move into their territory. They knew prosperity followed in Clifford's tracks and in any event, he was going to spend almost as much on the lifts as the government on the road.

Quebec's engineers started immediately to survey and plan the road. This was not enough for John when he was asked to start on the mountain. He reminded Fournier of the terms of his agreement: he would only start work on the lifts when road construction started, when earth and machinery were moving.

The contract for the road was given out to Normandin Construction in the spring of 1973, two years after the meeting with Fournier in Quebec City. "Not bad", said John to Milton Cross, as they watched the first bulldozers arrive outside the village of Cantley. The three mile road into Mont Cascades was under construction. Cross, knowing the speed of bureaucracy agreed. "Now it's our turn to put up," John reminded him.

John had not been idle; had made a proposal to the Department of Regional Expansion (DRE) and they had agreed to guarantee a loan of $600,000 when all the paperwork was signed. Mont Cascades was becoming a reality.

He was going to make a departure from his usual lift construction practise. While in Quebec city, he visited the manufacturing facility of Samson Lifts, a recently-established company. He was impressed with their work and their product. He was convinced by their engineer, Louis Handfield, the engineer who formerly worked with John when he sold and installed Poma lifts, that he should leave Poma and go with Samson. He agreed to represent Samson and built his first Samson chairlift and T-bar installation at Mont Cascades.

Milton Cross had not been idle either. The concept of a total development of ski hill and housing as described by John had impressed him. He owned 3000 acres of land along the side of the river at the mountain's base. His subdivision plans were prepared and he was ready to start capitalizing on all that was happening. John asked him to delay the lot sales until the ski hill was at a more advanced state of construction, arguing that the lots would increase substantially in value as the hill progressed. Cross did not want to wait; he wanted to start at once and told John that a Mr. Bill Brown would be taking care of all land sales; not John!

Brown had convinced Cross of his ability to do a better job in subdivision sales than John because of his past real estate sales experience. John was irritated, but there was little that he could do about it; Brown was going to market the real estate.

The first 200 lots sold before Cascades was open for business, and another 300 were eventually sold. They sold almost as fast as they were put up for sale. The ads that appeared in the Ottawa valley newspapers offering the "wilderness lots" were linked to John's name, lending credibility to the sales program. There would be skiing, golfing, even a marina. It was a real estate salesman's dream. At this time John was Cascade's developer-contractor and lift concessionaire; he had nothing to do with the sale of Cross' real estate nor did he profit from it in any way. Brown was simply trading on Clifford's name. When he learned of the killing that Brown was making on the lot sales, John had to ask himself if he was in the wrong end of the development business.

In past ski-area developments which he had been involved in, it had been important to use some of the profits from adjacent land sales to fund ski facility construction. With the corporate division of real estate and ski-area development, none of that type of financing was forthcoming. Since the mountain was the main draw, John felt it would be good business to ask Cross to put aside a percentage of his profits towards the area's construction. But Cross was satisfied with the sales arrangement that he had made with Brown and he was very satisfied with the work that John was doing to make it all possible. Why should he upset such a fine arrangement?

It was only after the first skiers were enjoying the Mont Cascades slopes when Bill Brown's sales started to drop off. Realizing that his sales needed a boost, he decided to institute one of John's techniques. He purchased (at a discount) $25,000 worth of season passes from John, which he used as an incentive to prospective lot purchasers. Had Brown agreed to the original request of lots-to-finance-hill construction, $500,000 would have been earned by the time the hill opened, DREE would have been off the hook, John clear of the bank and Brown and Cross could still have enjoyed a substantial profit.

An article written by Ottawa Journal reporter Michelle Morissette raised another issue. Brown was advertising and selling land on the western edge of Quebec. With his marketing aimed at Ottawa, most of the land that he sold was to "out-of-Quebec residents".

The article quotes Hull MNA Jocelynne Ouellette's reference to a study showing that "a high percentage of West Quebec's rural land is owned by non-residents." The article continued, "the study may be used in helping the provincial government develop its upcoming legislation controlling regional land purchasing." The western Quebec area's Outaouais Regional Development Council, a provincially subsidized agency, produced the report. They may have been prompted out of fear that Brown was selling Quebec off to Ontario citizens. Chairman Jean-Marie Seguin said, "a rational and coordinated plan for the growth of the region," grew from the study. John and his business of ski resort development was affecting the political scene.

One mile of the shoreline and 1100 acres of land immediately to the south of Mont Cascades was owned by a mining company with holdings throughout the world. It was no secret that the company, International Mogul Mines, also had a multi-million dollar bank account. It was also common knowledge throughout the mining investment community that they were in a no-win tax situation with the United

Kingdom. The mining corporation was compelled to pay millions of dollars to the UK. The accounting firm, Arthur Anderson Inc., a worldwide firm with head offices in Chicago, represented International Mogul Mines during the litigation.

The same accounting firm's office in Germany had a prominent businessman-sportsman client by the name of Baron Karl Von Wendt, a "Freiherr" man who could

Mont Cascades, Gatineau River in background. Bob Gratton's house on lower left, Clifford home lower left, North Side with triple chair lift on right, T-bar in centre, summer slide far left.

trace his lineage back to the year 1065. He was a sportsman, partaking in the sports of the elite. If he was not in Germany tending to his gigantic Theme Park business he most likely could be found racing fast boats and even faster cars somewhere in the world.

In the spring of 1975, Von Wendt was discussing his plans for opening a theme park in Canada with his accountants in Germany, when they told him of International Mogul Mines' problems and suggested that perhaps their property might become available at an interesting price.

Karl and his entourage of 8 or 10 people flew to Canada to look at the property and other parcels that Canadian realtors could offer him. He liked Canada, and even though his first choice of a property on 31-mile Lake was turned down by the Quebec Government, he elected to stay on. He bought a beautiful house on the Connor Estate, near Mont Cascades. The house, within sight of the ski slopes, suited him perfectly for his Canadian headquarters. His timing was politically less than perfect as he came in just as the Outaouais non-resident issue was coming to a boil.

Frustrated by the Quebec bureaucracy each time he put together a land purchase in the area, Von Wendt was about to look for greener pastures outside of Quebec when he met his neighbour, John Clifford. With Clifford's help, after extensive negotiations with the province, Von Wendt was able to purchase the Mogul Mines property. Having John on his side, and with the revelation that, when raising the capital to buy Mont Cascades, he had sold 20% of his interest to Mogul Mines International, it looked, at least from the outside, as if big business was moving in to develop Cascades. There was now a new 20% partner in Mont Cascades. A further investment of $200,000 bought out Milton Cross' share. Mont Cascades was now under 45% ownership by Baron Karl von Wendt's Two Seasons Company. With the purchase of The Mogul Mines property and his buy-out of Milton Cross, von Wendt had bought into the Gatineau for a one million dollars. And once again, for better or worse, John had a financially powerful partner.

Von Wendt did not get his Theme Park project going as quickly as he wished. However, in the interim, he was able to watch the progress of Mont Cascades' development. His 45% ownership in the resort was paying off, for four months of the year.

Just as John had found the answer to guaranteed snow throughout the ski season, Karl thought that he had the answer of what to do with a resort's idle summer months. He saw the lack of productivity, the down time, as a challenge and

The Clifford Summerslide was a profitable addition to the facilities at Mont Cascades

JOHN CLIFFORD

30

YEARS IN SKIING

Saturday, 27 March, 1976

A tribute to a man who has contributed

so much to skiing in Canada

A dinner and "roast" held in March 1976 to honour John's thirty years contribution to skiing, Eddie MacCabe as master of ceremonies.

he believed he had the answer in his theme park back in Germany.

John and Margaret were invited to Germany to visit Fort Fun, Karl Von Wendt's theme park. Among the many attractions of the park was a slide, modelled after the icy alpine Luge runs that were quite common throughout Europe. Snow was not necessary for Von Wendt's version of the slide. It was a summerslide with the cresta, a one-man molded fiberglass sled that sped down an asbestos and concrete trough on wheels instead of runners. The cresta could be slowed by the application of a brake controlled by the rider. The slide itself, the trough, could be as long as the property it was built on. It was a natural summer fill-in for any ski hill.

Von Wendt convinced John that Mont Cascades should have the first Summer Alpine Slide in North America and that John, through his connections, would become wealthy by selling and installing them in other ski centers across Canada. The slide was ready for business on Mont Cascades well before the the next winter's first snow fall.

"Clifford's Summerslide" was indeed the first of its kind in Canada. The giant slide offered a scenic six-minute chairlift ride up Mont Cascades with views of the Gatineau Hills and Ottawa's Parliament Buildings to the south; and then an exciting five minutes of twisting and turning down 2000 feet that curved through woods and over ski trails as it dropped 420 vertical feet. There was interest in the slide once Cascades' was in operation. Blue Mountain, Collingwood and Mont Gabriel in the Laurentians north of Montreal, were the next resorts to have the slide installed. With many more inquiries on his desk, John was once again feeling the rush of new development, of something else for the betterment of the ski industry.

Von Wendt's German and Canadian offices included a comptroller and advisor to oversee Karl's investments and operations. Al Ronneberger was a very shrewd businessman. He soon gained John's confidence and, with many a "don't worry John" that sounded vaguely familiar, he talked him into enlarging the facilities with another bar here, another restaurant there, all of which ran Cascades', and John's, debt up higher and higher.

As the debt grew, Ronneberger talked him into taking out a collateral mortgage on his house to help secure the increased debt. Ronneberger told John that he was confident that his new capital injection would result in higher profits for all.

The situation that John was now facing had a certain grim familiarity. Every ski area that he had been involved with, every development that he had put heart, soul and money into eventually fell into other hands. It looked as though it was about to happen again and he was powerless to prevent it. There was, however, a difference this time. He owned 55% of Mont Cascades; he was not a minority shareholder. However, he had to entertain Von Wendt's offer to buy him out, or end up with nothing.

Mont Cascades, a resort with multi-million dollar

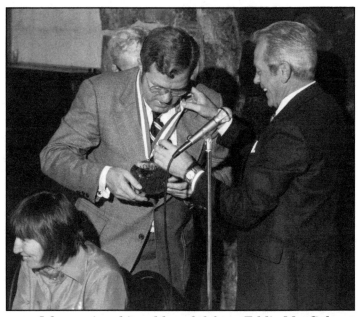

John receives his gold medal from Eddie MacCabe at the 30 year celebration.

potential, was slipping out of his grip. Meetings with his lawyers also proved to be of no avail; the advice was to accept Von Wendt's meagre offer of $500,000 to be paid in equal payments over the next 6 years. The only perk that went along with the deal was that John's house would be free and clear of any mortgage or liens. The year was 1978 - Clifford had given another five years of his life to the sport that he loved.

With skilled help from Dave Scott and Laird Rasmussen of Scott and Aylen, the buy-out was arranged. After the signing that completed the deal, Eddie MacCabe, the Ottawa Citizen's sports editor, said to John "And now there isn't another peak in the Gatineau worth developing."

"No," he answered, "I don't suppose there is. But even if there was, at this time in my life I don't think I'd be interested in tackling it." John returned to Ottawa, to his one-hill Carlington Park complex, never again to return to the Gatineau Hills that first saw him as a young skier 35 years before.

The Rusty Nail Gang: Howard McLaughlin, Bruce Wallace, John, Dan Drummond, Bob Cowley, Eric Tomlinson, Henri Robillard. Dave Scopie took the picture.

CHAPTER 21
On to Mount Pakenham

John had a soft spot in his heart for Carlington Park ski hill. He enjoyed watching youngsters gleefully taking their first sliding steps on skis. The skis might have been a gift from their parents, or may have been loaned by John if they could not otherwise afford them. He had conceived of the park as an incubator, and it truly was: many thousands of youngsters were taught to ski through the Kiwanis ski school and other clubs and schools using the Carlington facilities. But now, with his departure from Mont Cascades, the picture was about to change.

Even though the city of Ottawa owned Carlington Park, it did not assist in the park's financing. The responsibility was entirely John's and one that he didn't mind shouldering . . . when times were better. The little ski-hill with its single run was never a moneymaker. He had been subsidizing the operation for 12 years and, sadly, the day had come when he had to say, "I can't continue."

The accommodation at Carlington Park consisted of old, re-activated, but rarely refurbished, city-owned skating rink shacks. The pavillion that the city was to have provided had been shelved or otherwise side-tracked year after year. The shacks were very vulnerable to vandalism and theft and were constantly broken into. One week after the sale of Cascades the shacks were broken into for the fourth time that year; thieves broke through the doors and made off with $600 worth of equipment.

They also stole the park. It was the last season for the little ski-hill that had become an Ottawa winter landmark, and the nursery of many an Ottawa skier. That last theft was the final nail in the coffin; John did not open up the following season. Camp Fortune carried on running Carlington for two more seasons, and then gave it up. To Ottawa's loss, there was no one else willing to pick up the torch.

As far as the citizens of Ottawa knew, Carlington park just closed, never to re-open again. That, however, is not the whole story, as John recalls. "Obviously, I was not going to just walk away from my investment. I wanted to be bought out."

"I had Ron Carwardine appraise the equipment on the hill. His evaluation exceeded $150,000." The City hired Jeff White of Delta Engineering, John's major competitor in snowmaking installations, to do likewise. He came up with an evaluation of an impossible $95,000. It was his opinion that the snowmaking system needed modernizing. In John's opinion the snowmaking system was adequate for the hill. John was also surprised to hear that Mr.White had made an offer to the City to upgrade the snowmaking system for $50,000.

Mayor Marion Dewar offered John the option of either taking $95,000 for the equipment or remove it all from the hill at his expense. The offer was made on a take-it-or-leave-it basis and he was given only three days to reply. John chose the money. He had to consider his own future; he still had Mount Pakenham to fall back on, but it needed development.

Mount Pakenham.

In 1976, with the arrival to power of Rene Levesque's Partie Quebecois, John decided to leave Quebec. Management negotiations with Karl Von Wendt were coming to a satisfactory close; he was offered the position of manager for the next five years contingent on his selling all his Mont Cascades shares to Von Wendt.

It was like old times. John and Marg had just moved into their newly-completed house at Mont Cascades when he heard of another Ottawa area ski center that was in trouble. Former Camp Fortune night rider Russ Wilson and his partner Andy Davison were having financial difficulties at Mount Pakenham, just west of Ottawa. The Pakenham problems were compounded in the fall of 1977 when Davison died of a heart attack, leaving Wilson on his own to run and develop the area.

Before long Wilson realized that he wasn't up to the task. Learning that John was about to leave Mont Cascades, he arranged that they meet. Though John was still managing Mont Cascades, he was open to the offer of purchasing a part share in the Mount Pakenham operation. Having been bitten before, he would only consider a 51% ownership position. After extensive negotiation, a deal was struck giving John 50% ownership; however, when his payments were completed, in five years or less, he could exercise an option for a full 60% share of the resort. The signing of that deal in the winter of 1978 would bring John to the next step in his career, ownership of Mount Pakenham.

When John originally looked over the operation, he was astonished to find that Pakenham was only operating on Saturdays. A ski area open only one day of the weekend? There was rarely a Sunday that the hill could open because there was not enough money for staff; Mount Pakenham was on the verge of bankruptcy. With John as consultant, some necessary changes were made and the center survived the winter of 1978.

In the winter of 1979, John officially took over the area's operations. Unwilling to give up his home at Mont Cascades, he commuted daily to Pakenham. His first season went very well, in fact well enough to enable him to make the first of the five yearly payments that would eventually lead to his 60% ownership.

Within four years, with the sale of his house in Mont Cascades, John was in a position to move in full-time at Mount Pakenham. That move coincided with his final payment to Russ Wilson and Janet Davison, Andy's widow. Once more, however, a partner of John's was tempted to break a deal; his trusting way of doing business was about to burn him again!

With Mount Pakenham operating successfully, Russ Wilson no longer wanted to allow him to take up his option to buy the promised additional 10% ownership; John wondered whether anybody ever lived up to their word. The newly-built slopes and cross-country trails that John had installed were too tempting to the former management; they didn't want to let go. But John did not want to let go either; he wanted things to come out just as they were agreed when he stepped in to help save Mount Pakenham the few years before.

John Hamilton, of Hamilton and Appotive, a prominent Ottawa law firm, represented John, and the law offices of Soloway and Morin represented Russ Wilson. This time John did not feel that he was starting another race. He felt more as if he were arguing the results of a race after he had won.

The lawyers eventually came up with a solution that looked feasible and in fact to John's advantage. John was offered full ownership with the purchase of all of the remaining shares at a premium price. Fearlessly John accepted – now all he needed was the money. The Federal Business Development Bank, respecting his track record in the ski industry, provided the necessary funding to complete the purchase. He was now Mount Pakenham's major shareholder. This time, however, he was the major shareholder with a difference: the only other shares were held by Daughter Joanne and his accountant, Dick Cowan.

"This time I own 90 percent of it; I know this is it!" John said, in an interview with sportswriter Steve Madely. "Over there, we're going to put in two Quadruple chairlifts . . . over there, where those ponds are, we're going to build a lake . . . and when that's built . . ."

Mount Pakenham has become the model of all that John had been saying was necessary for the success of a ski center, no matter the vertical drop provided by nature. The perfect blend of recreational skiing, with a proper mix of peripheral housing and services, is the key to ski area prosperity.

Today, with its quadruple chair and the upgrading of the existing facilities, the enlarged lodge, improved hills, cross-country trails, snowmaking and lighting, Mount Pakenham can lay claim to being the most modern ski resort in eastern Ontario. And, true to John's belief that the youngster, the skier of the future, holds the key to the future of the ski industry, Mount Pakenham continues to enlarge its ski school and its Skiing in Schools program.

By definition, a family ski center is an area providing all the facilities for a family to ski together and to play together. Such an area will have beginner, intermediate, and expert slopes allowing for a natural progression as the individual's ability develops. The prime factor that defines a family ski center, however, is the overall vertical drop, the topography of the site itself. There will be enough of a drop for a thrill, testing the skiers ability while allowing the improvement of technique with little danger to life and limb. John Clifford's Mount Pakenham is just such an area.

Each winter Mount Pakenham has more than 100 instructors giving lessons to more than 15,000 children. John will often be found on the slopes watching his skiers in action. "Many of the children's parents started skiing with the Kiwanis program," he says. "Whenever a parent comes up to me and tells me that he or she started on the old Carlington Park hill, or at Beamish, I feel tremendously proud. I feel that they are part of my family. I will never forget those early days. The children learned so easily and they had so much fun." Looking about, he says, "And they still do."

John may not remember the names of all those skiers but few of them will forget him and his athletic family. Skiers and many others will never forget his daughter Betsy, who, by the time she retired in 1976, had put together a very impressive record.

Betsy, herself now a mother of four, credits her father's inspiration as the chief factor in her skiing success. "My father's determination to overcome, his drive to win, was instilled in me from the age of five, when he schooled and coached me on Camp Fortune's hills. He gave me the courage and the mental attitude to be a winner."

Unfortunately for Betsy, and for Canada, her career coincided with a time of turmoil in Canadian skiing. A coaching philosophy copied from the Green Bay Packer's Vince Lombardi conflicted with the essentially individual nature of skiing competition. A fiercely independant competitor, Betsy came into conflict with the anti-individualist team philosophy at every turn. She was travelling the world in her early teens without a companion, mentor, or chaperon to provide personal support. There was also no provision for helping her keep up with school work. As a consequence, she withdrew on several occasions, frustrated, and eventually retired from competitive skiing in 1976, at the age of 22.

John's correspondence and meetings with I.C.C. Chairman Eddie Creed and Alpine Program Director Al Raine reveal a fundamental disagreement about the best way to handle Betsy's career. Since that time, it has become commonplace for athletes of Betsy's stature to have support staff and managers of their own to ensure they fulfil their athletic promise. But Betsy was coping with international competition, stardom and all the accompanying social pressures, virtually alone. John's repeated requests that the team provide a companion fell on deaf ears.

Betsy winning the World Cup Slalom in Schruns, Austria in 1973.
She was 19.

In spite of all the factors working against her, Betsy's career was phenomenal. At 16, she was the youngest person ever to capture a World Championship (Val Gardena, Italy, 1970). She was the downhill silver medalist at the 1974 World Championships, and placed 12 times in the top ten in World Cup races. Two of those wins were slalom gold medals. Ironically, in 1974, her silver medal was won at St. Moritz, goal of her father's abortive Olympic drive.

It is tempting to speculate what might have been, if Betsy had received appropriate support and guidance at those crucial times. "Betsy has always been willful and headstrong," says her father. "I know she was a hell of a handful for her coaches on occasion. But I think that goes with her will to win. Trying to break her spirit out of some mistaken idea of team discipline undermined her ability to compete."

Joanne, Betsy's sister, is a chartered accountant. She too is an ardent skier; she was brought up on the slopes of her father's many ski developments. Her main involvement in the sporting world is through her partnership in Wilderness Tours, a white water rafting adventure business.

The Clifford's youngest daughter, Susan, now lives in England. She was a National Ski Team member and world cup racer who, upon leaving amateur racing, went on to become one of the best in the ladies North American professional racing circuit.

John and Marg's son, Stephen, was killed in a dune buggy accident at Camp Fortune in September, 1970. He was 13 years old.

There have been many articles and stories published about John Clifford throughout his career. The sportswriters and broadcasters attached many a label to his name; Canada's One Man Ski Team; The Skier; The King of Skiing. Federal Court Justice Marcel Joyal, one of the four original backers of Mont Ste. Marie called him a Lovable Rascal when at one of the numerous occasions honouring John. He described him as a man with "the greatest of personal integrity; however, he could manipulate as no one else I know. You have to love him." John does not necessarily like to be labelled, but he does appreciate being thought of in a kindly way for his contribution to the building and promotion of skiing as a sport and a business. He considers himself to be a builder, a developer, a teacher.

"The Ottawa area has the highest concentration of skiers per capita of any region in North America," says John. "I've dedicated most of my life to making it so, but there's no way I could have done it alone. Fifty-five years ago the Ottawa Senators folded and left a vacuum, and skiing filled the gap.

Betsy with her parents, arriving home after winning the World cup Giant Slalon an 1970. She was 16.

Betsy at Mont Ste. Marie with her boyfriend Jean Guay, John Clifford in pursuit.

"Jack Koffman and Bob Mellor at the Ottawa Citizen, and Bill Westwick and Eddie McCabe at the Ottawa Journal got behind me as skiing was growing so fast. McCabe had a half-hour ski show on the CBC on Saturday mornings.

"We offered free ski lessons to the Ottawa Roughriders every Monday night. Ronnie Stewart, Russ Jackson, Kaye Vaughan, Whit Tucker, Gilles Archambault, they skiied all winter. It helped build a great esprit de corps among the football players, made them a great team, and it was great publicity for skiing. We had Roughriders-versus-the media ski competition every year. The media team was led by Eddie McCabe and Bob Mellor. The Roughriders beat the pants off them. The Ottawa area was made up of doers, not viewers, and 200,000 skiers is the result."

On March 18, 1982, the Board of Directors of the Canadian Ski Museum invited

1991: Inauguration into the Laurentian Ski hall of Fame. John, Martha McKeena, Alexander Kerr Gillespie, Georges Vigeant, Roger Monast.

John revisiting Portillo, Chile, sitting with the current owners, Henry and David Purcell, 1973.

John to the inaugural dinner of the Honour Roll of Canadian Skiing. The Honour Roll, the first of it's kind, is dedicated to those who have contributed extraordinarily to the development of skiing in Canada.

The letter of invitation stated that John had been elected from a list of nominations received from a nationally-appointed committee with members located in several parts of Canada. Mr. Rae Grinnell, the Museum's Chairman told the dinner guests, "John has acted as consultant on ski development to the federal government, and to every provincial government east of British Columbia." He went on to say, "The nominating committee has made a wise choice in electing John Clifford to the Honour Roll as he indeed has done his bit not only in the Gatineau but across the Nation as well."

More recently in October 1991, the Quebec Musee du Ski elected John to their Temple de la Renommee. John received the honour at a gala dinner held at the Mont Gabriel Lodge. In his acceptance speech he told his fellow guests that it was gratifying for him to see that the above-ground pipes of the snowmaking system that he installed over 30 years ago were still in operating condition, as was the summerslide that he had also installed. He then said with a sly grin, "If I'd known then of built-in obsolescence,I might now be a very rich man." Roger Monast, the museum's president, presented a plaque to John with the words that loosely translated mean that they hoped John, too, would last as long as his many installations in Quebec.

Perhaps John should be a millionaire, even a multi-millionaire. He is not. John Clifford is not the typical entrepreneur, driven by dollars. He is a sportsman, driven by the love of sport. In particular the sport of skiing.

Today John and Marg Clifford continue to make skiing more accessible and financially viable for the average skier. Now 70, he continues to work as hard as ever. The Cliffords' dream is to develop Pakenham into a year-round resort area, and it is well on its way. The first nine holes of a golf course are well beyond the planning stage and six homes have already been built in the first phase of a 223-lot subdivision around the proposed golf course.

"I've had a lot of fun in the past 48 years," says Mr. John Frederick Clifford. "Why quit now?"

PHOTO BY SHEILA STATHAM

In the rental shop at Mount Pakenham.

*J.P. Chasse et Peche:
Pat Cashman,
Mickey Romhild,
Lucien Raymond,
Gerry Slobodian,
John Clifford,
Spud Murphy.*

Right: John with Sal Pantalone and Doug MacDonald at Chubb Cay in the Bahamas, with a 325 lb. marlin, 1987.

Below: On Lake Ontario with Doug MacDonald. Trips with the Ottawa-Carleton Fish and Game Club took John to Greenland, Alaska, Labrador, Newfoundland, and the Carribean.

ACHIEVEMENTS AND HONOURS OF JOHN CLIFFORD

Athletic Achievements

1945	Rowing Association Regatta – Ottawa Rowing Club Stroked 5 winning events
1946	First, Ski Union of the Americas - Chile
1947	Second, Canadian Alpine Ski Championships, Mont Ste. Anne, Que.
1948	First, Central Canada Cross-Country Championships Alternate, Canadian Olympic Ski Team
1949	First, Central Canada Alpine Combined First, Canadian Closed Alpine Championships, Mont Tremblant, Que.
1950	Canadian F.I.S. team, Aspen Colorado
1951	First, Quebec Division Slalom Championships, Val Cartier, Que.
1952	Alternate, Canadian Olympic Ski Team
1953 1954	First, Quebec Provincial Waterski Championships Sixth Overall, World Waterski Championships, CNE Toronto First, Quebec Provincial Waterski Championships
1955	First, Canadian Waterski Championships, CNE Toronto First, Quebec Provincial Waterski Championships
1956	First, Canadian Closed Alpine Ski Championships, Collingwood, Ontario First, Quebec Provincial Waterski Championships

Technical Achievements

Started eight ski schools, starting with Kiwanis Ski School.

Built twenty ropetows, assisted by Steve Saunders.

Installed sixty-five snowmaking systems across Canada

Introduced Thiokol, Flextrac and Bombardier grooming machines, powder-maker and rollers from Valley Engineering

Supplied and installed Poma and Samson lifts across Canada.

Installed first double chairlift in Eastern Canada

First all-steel T-bar in Canada, 1956

Installed night skiing 1949 at Beamish Hill and at Ladies Ski School, Camp Fortune

Introduction of Alpine Slide at Mont Cascades, Blue Mountain, Bromont, Mont Gabriel and Twilicum Valley, B.C.

Development Achievements

Camp Fortune

Beamish Hill

Mont Tremblant, North Side

Mont Ste. Marie

Mont Cascades

Mt. Pakenham

Calabogie Peaks, assisted Bill Hodgins

Consulted in development of many ski areas across Canada

Honours

1956	Ottawa's Outstanding Amateur Athlete
1982	Honour Roll of Canadian Skiing, Canadian Ski Museum Ottawa Sports Hall of Fame
1991	Laurentian Ski Musem Hall of Fame
1993	Canadian Ski Instructor's Alliance Hall of Fame

ABOUT THE AUTHORS

John A. Stevens is a freelance writer and editor based in Toronto. He has edited numerous books of biography, fiction and non-fiction and is the author of three plays for young people. He and his family of seven divide their time between Toronto, the Ottawa Valley and the Annapolis Valley in Nova Scotia.

Elliott Kaufmann is an avid skier, ski patroller, artist and writer. He lives in Lac Guindon, Quebec.

A note from Elliott Kaufmann:

Creating the original manuscript for this book has been a rewarding and exciting experience. Many hours were spent at Mount Pakenham taping dozens of interviews and sorting through reams of his unpublished memoirs. The more we talked, the more I read, the better I got to know this remarkable man.

Although John is well known to people associated with skiing in Eastern Ontario, few know of the impact that he has had on the ski industry as a whole, throughout Canada and indeed the world. I had, through the process, the privilege of getting to know John intimately, furthering our mutual desire to tell his story.

My task could not have been done without the significant cooperation of many wonderful people drawn together by their affection for the incredible John Clifford and by their love of skiing. I am particularly indebted to May Arbess for her encouragement and the many hours she spent at the keyboard of her word processor.

I know, as you read on, you will learn, as I did, how John Clifford was a man of his times and how he in fact fashioned those times.

Elliott Kaufmann

APPENDIX: THE PEOPLE IN THE BOOK

Peter Ackroyd
Danny Ackroyd
Emille Allais
Georgette Allais
Vic Allen
Hortense Anba
Arthur Anderson
Franz Baier
Ron Baillie
Bill Ball
Battista
Lyle Beamish
Pierre Beaudin
Gabby Beaudry
Rollie Beaudry
Bill Beck
Colin Berg
John Bergeron
Tito Belledonne
Paul Berniquez
Jacques Berniquez
Jim Bisson
George Boivin
Charlie Boland
Phil Bott
Real Breton
Don Britt
George Brittain
Fred Bronson
Bill Brown
John Buck
Dieter Bührle
Bernie Bureau
Don Bohart
Pat Cashman
Elmer Cassel

John Carscadden
Bud Clark
Ernie Clarke
Gary Clarke
Betsy Clifford
Bob Clifford
Fred Clifford
Florence Clifford
Mary Clifford
Harvey Clifford
Joanne Clifford
Stephen Clifford
Susan Clifford
Denise Colson
Marianne Colson
DeeDee Colson
Jane Colson
Bob Cowley
Jeff Crain
Ted Crain
Milton Cross
Linda Crutchfield
Eddie Creed
Alf Dulude
Marcel D'Amour
Sydney Dawes
Guy Debassecourt
Gilbert Dedardel
Gordy Dean
Joe Dodge
Chalo Dominguez
Fritz Dubach
Fred Dixon
Hubert Douglas
Dan Drummond
Charlie Duncan

Peter Duncan
Kay Durocher
Augustine Edwards
Jean Errazuriz
Frank Elkins
George Encil
Ray Everly
Aurele Faubert
Harold Fawcett
Roy Fournier
Bruce Fleming
Glen Fraser
John Fripp
Ginny Fripp
Shawn Fripp
Clarence Fuller
Fred Foster
Bernie Garand
Jim Georges
Henry Gill
Alex Kerr Gillespie
George Gowling
Bob Gratton
Rae Grinnell
Ted Gordon
Gordon Grant
George Grossman
Jean Guay
Louis Handfield
Fred Hall
Arturo Hammersley
Fred Hanna
John Hanna
Wilf Harris
Alan Hay
George Hees

Bill Hodgins
Dave Hyman
Anne Heggtveit
Alex Hussey
John Irvin
Bill Irving
Bob Irving
Lucien Isabelle
Pierre Jalbert
Philip Jenner
Peter Jessen
Howard Johnson
Marcel Joyal
Bud Keenan
Peter Kingsmill
Christopher Klotz
Jack Koffman
Guy Laframboise
Rejean Lafreniere
Wy Lawson
Bert Lawrence
Sigurd Lockeberg
Vince Lombardi
Gabriel Loubier
Paul Lajoie
Ron Leafloor
Reg Lefebvre
Jean Lesage
Art Lovett
Art Levine
Eddie MacCabe
Alex MacDonald
Doug MacDonald
Harold Mahlavski
Ralph Mallory
Herbert Marshall

135

John Matthewson
Ernie McCulloch
Alex McDougall
George McHugh
Frank McIntyre
Martha McKeena
Howard McLaughlin
Harry McLean
Ken Meikle
Bob Mellor
Roger Monast
Odd Michaelson
Michelle Morrissette
Fred Morris
C.E. Mortureaux
Spud Murphy
Jack Noonan
Ken Nolan
Bob O'Billovich
Brian O'Brien
Helen O'Connell
Nano Oelckers
Jocelynne Oellette
Alex O'Nosko
Jim O'Reilly
Henri Orrelier
Sal Pantalone
Stew Parsons
Oswald Parent
James Patrick
Earl Pearlman
Joe Philippe
Art Pineault
Fernand Perriard
Arturo Podesta
Margaret Phillips
Eddy Phillips
Bill Petersen
Henry Purcell

David Purcell
Hamilton Quain
Redmond Quain Sr.
Redmond Quain Jr.
Al Raine
Laird Rasmussen
Lucien Raymond
Don Reid
Hans Rechsteiner
Walter Roach
Fred Richardson
Claude Richer
Henri Robbillard
Daniel Rochon
Mickie Romhild
Al Ronneberger
Herb Rushleau
Mary Ryan
Joe Ryan
Jake Robbins
Steve Saunders
George Schmidt
Dave Scopie
Russel Smart
Helen Saunders
Fred Sharp
Dave Scott
Jim Scott
Fred Sharp
Pat Sligh
Gerry Slobodian
Vera Stepan
Hector Stephanie
Ronnie Stewart
Tony Smialowski
Peter Sneyd
Rheal Seguin
Stig Sjolund
Percy Sparks

Harold Taggart
Lowell Thomas
Bill Tindale
Art Tommy
Andy Tommy
Eric Tomlinson
John P. Taylor
John Turner
Reg Toomey
Joe Tropeano
Phil Tropeano
Ralph Thornton
Georges Vanier
John Veit
Bill Vant
Digby Viets
George Vigeant
Bruce Wallace
Knobby Walsh
Wally White
Jeff White
Bill Walsh Jr.
Bob Wallace
Bill Westwick
Karl Von Wendt
Franz Williamson
Ross Walker
Tor Wiebust
Dave Wright
Charlotte Whitton
Percy Wood
Dalton Wood
Allan Wotherspoon
Father Zachary